KULACUDAMANI NIGAMA

KULACUDAMANI NIGAMA

ARTHUR AVALON

AND

AKSAYA KUMAR MAITRA

Published by

GYAN

Gyan Publishing House
5, Ansari Road
Daryaganj, New Delhi-110002
Phone: 011-47034999, 9811692060
E-mail: books@gyanbooks.com

Distribution Network
gyanbooks.com
India, USA, Canada, UK, Australia

ISBN: 978-93-6920-318-5 (PB)

First Published, 1956

2nd Impression 2025

Printed at: Gyan Press, Delhi.

KULACUDAMANI NIGAMA
Author: ARTHUR AVALON and AKSAYA KUMAR MAITRA

॥ कुलचूडामणि तन्त्रम् ॥

KULACŪDĀMANI NIGAMA

EDITED BY
ARTHUR AVALON

श्री

PREFACE

'Kulacudāmaṇi' is one of the shortest Tantras relating to the Śakta Āgama School of Hindu Religion. It deals exclusively with the Kaula Ācara or doctrine which is claimed to be the most superior form of worship. It is doubtful whether this Tantra as it is now published is complete or whether it is only a portion of a still larger work. As it is, it is not an exhaustive treatise on any particular school or Devata or Mantra. Although Dakṣina Kāli is expressed to be the guiding and predominant Devi in Chap. IV, neither Her Mantra nor Tantra nor avarana devatas nor form of worship is expounded in the work. Only the last chapter (Chap. VII) deals with Mahisa Mardani with some detail and stotra and worship of Mahisha Mardani is just mentioned. The doctrine and tenets of Kaula Ācāra on which it is said to be an authoritative treatise, are not fully dealt with as in Kulārnava, Jnānārnava, Tantra-rāja and other leading tantras of the school. It would appear as if it is a small portion of an exhaustive treatise, the full text of which is not available.

Kula Cūdāmaṇi, as explained in the Introduction means the 'Crown Jewel' of 'Kula' doctrine and the term 'Kula' has been explained to represent Śakti in Her Triputi aspect of Matri, Mana and Meya. But it may be noted that 'Kula' also denotes the Mūlādhāra, the Padma where the Tattva of Earth is absorbed (Ku = earth ; Liyate Atra = is absorbed or Kum Lati), the abode of Śakti and the starting point of Suṣumna Nadi and the connected Kula-Sahasrāra below Mūlādhāra. (Vide the commentary of Bhāskararāya 'Soubhagya Bhāskara' on Lalita Sahasranāma on verses 87 and 88 beginning with "Kulamritaika rasika" and the names Kundalini, Kuleswari, Kulakundalaya, Kaulamārga Parasevita and Kaulinikevala etc. The word 'Cūdāmaṇi', the crown or crown-Jewel also means the crown or head of Kula, the top-most terminus of Suṣumna, the Akula Sahasrāra Padma at the top of the head, the abode of Siva. The Tantra deals with 'Kula' and 'Kulacūda' or 'Kula cūdāmaṇi' (Kulasya cha and Kulacūdāmaṇescha Tantra) or with Kula and Akula i. e., Śakti and Śiva in Sāmarasya (blissful union) and the down-ward flow of Kulāmrita for purpose of creation or cosmic ideation (Prapanca) and the final rest of Śakti in her abode. The Tantra which deals with this essential doctrine of Kaula Ācāra is Kula Cūdāmaṇi Tantra.

Sri Śankaracharya in verses 9 & 10 of Anandalahari beginning with 'Mahim Mulādhāre' and 'Sudhadharasaraih' describes exactly the aspect of Kula or Kundalini yoga, the essence of Kaulācāra. Sri Goudapādācārya in his 'Subhagodaya Stuti'. V-7, says "The Kaulas assert that the Trikona (in Mūlādhāra) is the Kulagriha i.e., the abode of Śakti ; some others say it is the square ; while the Samayins locate the place of Śakti in the Bindu (the Akula Sahasrara in the head)" The apparent conflict between the two accepted great Ācāras (doctrines), Samaya and Kaula seems to be in the conception or experience of the functioning of Śakti. As sound or energy travels in ripples or circular waves, the Kaulas, more analytically state that the starting point of the sound or energy i. e., Mūlādhāra is the abode of Śakti while the Samayins experiencing its expansion and Sāmarasya with Siva state that the terminal point in the Bindu is the abode of Śakti. In fact there is no fundamental difference of opinion between the two schools of thought and the apparent difference is due only to different kinds of yogic experience.

In this work, although the tenets, principles and practice of Kaulācāra are not expounded in detail, the essence of the doctrine is laid down in the eleven verses, after the enumeration of the several Tantras, wherein the three states or stages of Śakti are described. The first is the primordial quiescent static state where the Śakti is one with Śiva in blissful union (Sāmarasya or Prakritirupa Cidānanda parayana) without attributes or form described by Sri Śankara in verse 9 of Ānandalahari. It is the state of Nirguna or Niṣkala Brahman mentioned in Sārada Tilaka, Kulārnava etc. and the Ānandamaya Kośa of Advaita School. The second state or stage is that when the Devi, veiling Herself with her own Maya, becomes intent on creation and assumes the three-fold aspect of Matri, Mana, Meya blended into one. This is the Sakala state or the Vijnānamayakosa. The next or 3rd stage is that of cosmic ideation (Bahancha) and the conception of the creation of the trinity, the world and so on.

These two stages are described by Sri Śankara in verse 10 of Ānandalahari. It is this Kaula doctrine that is fully expounded in Kāmakalāvilāsa of Punyānanda, more particularly in sutras 1 to 8 known as Turiyapada or Avidya Pada.

Although this work is not exhaustive, it is accepted as one of the authoritative treatises on Kadi

Mata and Kaulācāra and is ranked equally with Kulārnava, Kalivilāsa & others. Messrs Ganesh & Company (Madras) Private Ltd., in republishing some of these obscure and misjudged treatises dealing with highly metaphysical and spiritual doctrines of Hindu Religion are doing a great service to the cause of the revival of interest in the religious and philosophical literature of the country.

Visakhapatnam
November 1956.

KARRA RAMAMURTHY

Corrections in print of the Text:

Third Patala, Verse 13, page 11, line 6. For 'वान्तान्ते' substitute 'बालांन्ते' (Bālānte) and in verse 14, page 11, line 8 - कुरु for गुरु. The mantra is ऐंक्लीं सौ : त्रिपुरायैं नमः इमां शक्ति पवित्रं कुरुं, मम शक्तिं कुरु स्वाहा - of 26 letters.

INTRODUCTION

This first edition of the hitherto unpublished Kulacūdāmaṇi has been prepared with the help of manuscripts (marked क and ख) collected by the Varendra Anusaṁdhāna Samiti of Rajshahi from reputed centres of Tāntrika worship in Bengal. The text has been compared in several cases with other manuscripts access to which was given by Tāntrika Gurus to the travelling Pandit of the Samiti. The work consists of seven Patalas (chapters). This Tantra is of a different type from that published in the Prapancasāra Tantra.

The Kulacūdāmaṇi-tantra or "crest-jewel" of the Kulācāra division of Tāntrika Sādhakas is included in the list of revealed works, which, according to the Vāmakeśvara-Tantra, are considered to be the chief amongst those which deal with the worship of Śakti. It is accordingly found frequently referred to as an authority in many compilations though the Kulacūdāmaṇi itself (II. 8) refers us, for all technical terms, to the Bhairavi-Tantra, which is, however now known chiefly from quotations made from it.

Like all original works on Tāntrika worship, the Kulacūdāmaṇi is cast in the form of a dialogue—the Sāstra being revealed by the Devī in Her form as Bhairavī, in answer to questions put to Her by Śiva in His form as Bhairava. For this reason the book is included in the class which goes by the name of *Nigama as opposed to Āgama*, in which the Śāstra is revealed by Śiva Himself. The form in which a Śāstra is presented whether as the Revelation of Śiva or Śakti is mere Līlā, since Śiva and Śakti are one and the same and it is Śiva who reveals. Siva is the revealer of the Śāstra in all cases, though in some He figures as Śiṣya and in others as Guru. The Svacchanda-Tantra puts this clearly in the following verse :

गुरुशिष्यपदे स्थित्वा स्वयमेव महेश्वरः ।
प्रश्नोत्तरपदैर्वाक्यैस्तन्त्रं समवतारयत् ॥

Guru śiṣyapade sthitvā svayameva maheśvaraḥ.
Praśnottara-padair vākyaistantraṁ samavatārayat.

The Tantra according to this verse, was originally revealed by Maheśvara (Śiva) who Himself stood for that purpose in the position of the Guru as well as that of the Śiṣya. This is also stated in the last chapter (VII. 79) of the Kulacūdāmaṇi where the Devi addressing Her Lord says :—

Gurustvam sarvatantrāṇām. (गुरुस्त्वं सर्वतन्त्राणाम्)

Kulācāra has been called a secret doctrine and practice. The Bhairavi in discoursing of it in the Kulacūdāmaṇi says at the outset (I. 31) that it had not been told to Viṣṇu nor to Brahma nor to Gaṇapa.

Kaula knowledge, says the text (II. 25) must not be divulged to atheists, fools, Pasus, or to enemies. The secret teaching appears to have been transmitted for a long time "from mouth to mouth" (Vaktrat vaktrāntaraṁ— वक्त्राद्वक्त्रान्तरम्) and even when it came in part to be reduced into writing, sufficient precaution was taken to conceal it from the uninitiated under technical terms, the import of which could only be learnt from the Guru. The general features may, however, be summed up as follows.

Although the word Kula in ordinary parlance means a family or clan, its technical sense has been defined by the

Tārārahasyavārttika to be "Kulaṁ-matṛ-māna-meyaṁ." The term thus combines the meaning of the three other words which are further explained to mean Jīva (Mātā) Jnāna (Mānaṁ) and the manifold universe or Viśva (Meyaṁ). The gist (Saṁkalitārtha) therefore is said to be Śakti. As Śakti is Kula so Śiva (as distinguished from Śakti) is spoken of as Akula. Kulācāra is one of the seven Acarās enumerated by the Kulārṇava one of the leading Tantras of the division of Sādhakas of this school called Kaulas. According to the last named Tantra it occupies the highest rank. "The Vaidikācāra" it says, "is no doubt higher than all, but Vaisṇavācāra is higher than Vaidikācāra; Śaivācāra is higher than Vaiṣṇavācāra; Dakṣiṇācāra is higher than Śaivācāra; Vāmācāra is higher than Dakṣiṇācāra; Siddhāntācāra is higher than the last and Kulācāra is superior to all.

As Kulācāra is thus said to be the highest of the Ācāras, only those Sādhakas are qualified therefor who in this or another birth have graduated in the preceding Ācāras which are regarded as stepping stones to it. Such a Sādhaka is called Kaulika or Kulīna. Being the final stage of Sādhana this Ācāra knows no distinction of race, colour, caste or sect. But the esoteric character of its doctrine and practice is such that it was never meant for the ordinary man of the world. On the contrary the difficulties of its true practice are said to be such that according to the doctrine "it is easier to walk on a drawn sword," than to be a true Kaula. It is expressly stated (I. 42) that the Adhikārī must be a Kulīna that is one who is capable of realizing that every person, thing, and act is a manifestation of the Mother or Śakti (Strīmayaṁ ca jagatsarvaṁ-स्त्रीमयं च जगत्सर्वम्). An essential feature of this Ācāra is the attainment of the knowledge that the Mother who is worshipped under different forms as Tripurā, Kālikā and so forth with differing rituals is She from whom all creation proceeds and who is all in all. This is very aptly set forth in the text (I. 24) which says "Oh All-knowing One, if Thou knowest Me then of what use are the Āmnāyas (revealed teachings) and Yajanaṁ (sacrifices : ritual)? If Thou knowest Me not, then of what use are Āmnāya and Yajanaṁ?"

This teaching has found its way into popular Bengali songs which say.

यदि मां विद्धि सर्वज्ञ क चाम्नायः क याजनम् ।
न विद्धि मां चेत्सर्वज्ञ क चाम्नायः क याजनम् ॥

Yadi mām viddhi sarvajna kva cāmnayah kva yājanaṁ.
Na viddhi maṁ cet sarvajna kva camnayah kva yājanaṁ.

"Tell me what will japa, tapa, yoga and yāga do for a man in whom Kulakuṇḍalini awakens and for the man in whom She awakens not." Supremacy is claimed for Kulācāra on the ground that it is the final stage of Sādhana in which Knowledge is realised to be superior to ritual. Kuladharma is accordingly said to weigh more than all Yājnas and Vratas put together in the scale against it though such rituals are necessary in the preliminary Ācāras which qualify for the last. As jnāna alone secures liberation the Kulārṇava-Tantra affirms that without Kuladharma liberation is not possible. With the question whether this claim is well founded I am not concerned but with the statement of the historical facts. As being the Ācāra which is claimed to be at the entry of liberation it is regarded by Kaulas as supreme and the end for those which precede it. Other schools take a different view of the Kaula claims.

CHAPTER I.

The book opens with an enumeration of the Kulasundaris or Devis who are said to be innumerable, under the names of Tripurā, Kālikā, Vāgiśvarī, Sukulā, Kulā, Mataṅginī, Pūrṇā, Vimalā, Caṇḍanāyikā, Ekajatā, Durgā and others. Several doctrines also such as Vaiṣṇava, Gāṇapatya and others are mentioned.

The names of a number of Tantras belonging to the sixty-four are next given. A complete list has been quoted in the foot-notes from the Vāmakeśvara-tantra, according to which each of the eight Bhairavas has a Tantra of his own, all of which are collectively known as the Bhairavāṣṭakaṁ. Similarly the Tantras relating to the seven Mātṛkās and the Śivadūtīs are collectively called Bahūrūpāṣṭakam. The Yāmalas are eight in number. These three classes give us 24 works, while the rest are those named in the list.

The 64 Tantras given in the Vāmakeśvara are as follows :—

1—4 Mahāmāyā - Śaṁbara, Yoginījāla - Śaṁbara ; Tattva-Śaṁbara.

5—12 Bhairavāṣṭaka — (*a*) Asitānga, (*b*) Ruru (*c*) Caṇḍa, (*d*) Krodha, (*e*) Uṇmatta, (*f*) Kapāli, (*g*) Bhīṣaṇa, (*h*) Saṁhāra.

13—20 Bahurūpāṣṭaka—the eight Tantras of the seven Mātṛkās and Śivadūtīs;

21—28 Yāmalāṣṭaka—(*a*) Brahmayāmala, (*b*) Viṣṇuyāmala, (*c*) Rudrayāmala, (*d*) Lakṣmīyāmala, (*e*) Umāyāmala, (*f*) Skandayāmala—(Bhāskara substitutes Jayadrathayāmala), (*g*) Gaṇeśayāmala, (*h*) Grahayāmala.

*29 Mahocchuṣya
*30 Vātūla
*31 Vātūlottara
32 Hṛdbheda
*33 Tantrabheda
34 Guhyatantra
35 Kāmika
36 Kalāvāda
37 Kalāsāra
38 Kubjikāmata
*39 Tantrottara
40 Vīṇātantra
41 Trodala
42 Trodalottara
43 Pancāmṛta
44 Rūpabheda
45 Bhūtoddāmara
46 Kulasāra
47 Kuloḍḍiśa
*48 Kulacūḍāmaṇi
49 Sarvajnānottara
*50 Mahākālīmata
51 Mahālakṣmimata
52 Siddhayogeśvarīmata
53 Kurūpikāmata
54 Devarūpikamata
55 Sarvavīramata
56 Vimalāmata
57(*a*) Purvāmnāya
(*b*) Paścimāmnāya
(*c*) Dakṣiṇāmnāya
(*d*) Uttarāmnāya
58 Niruttara
59 Vaiśeṣika
60 Jnānārṇava
61 Vīrāvali
62 Aruṇeśa
63 Mohinīśa
64 Viśuddheśvara

It has not been found possible to identify with certainty all items in the list given in this work with that of the Vāmakeśvara and in some respects the list differs. If however, we take Māyottara, Kalāpaka or Kalāpada, Sarvajnānātmaka and Viśuddheśvara which occur in the

Kulacūdāmaṇi to refer to items 1, 36, 48, and 64 respectively of the Vāmakeśvara list then the two lists correspond except as to the 9 items marked with an asterisk. In the place of these last the present work appears to give the names of the following Tantras :—Mahāsārasvata, Tantrajnāna, Vāsuki, Mahāsammohana, Mahāsūkṣma, Vāhana, Vāhanottara, Mātṛbheda, Viśvātmaka, Śivāvali. If, however, we thus count them we get 10 Tantras or one too many. Possibly Mahāsūkṣma may be part of the title of the Vāhana Tantra which succeeds it, in which case it may be eliminated.

Bhairava then says that He knows all these Kulasundaris, doctrines, and Tantras but has nevertheless not attained bliss (Ānanda). He asks Bhairavī why this is so.

In reply Bhairavī first gives some general philosophical instructions in eleven verses (I. 16-26) to Bhairava whom She addresses as the most Supreme Kula, the ocean of Tāntrika Kula knowledge (Tantrajnāna-kulārṇava) which, since He apparently seeks instruction, has for the moment been obscured by Her Māyā. This portion may be divided into three sections. The first (vv. 16-17) refers to that primordial state when She as Prakṛti was hidden in Cidānanda (Ahaṁ Prakṛtirūpā ceccidānandaparāyaṇa—अहं प्रकृतिरूपा चेच्चिदानन्दपरायणा.) In this state there is neither creation, maintenance nor destruction ; neither Brahma, Hari, Śaṁbhu nor other Devas ; neither attachment, suffering nor liberation ; neither piety, Theism, Atheism, Japa, Guru nor Śiṣya.

The second state (vv. 17-24) is that in which the Devi covering Herself with Her own Māya becomes desirous of creation (Unmukhī) and threefold. Then joyful in the mad delight which comes of Her union with the Supreme Akula She becomes Vikāriṇī; that is the Vikāras or Tattvas arise in Mūlaprakṛti.

माययाच्छाद्य चात्मानं त्रिधा भूत्वा यदोन्मुखी ।
पराकुलरसोन्मादमोदिनी च विकारिणी ॥

Māyayācchādya cātmānaṁ tridhā bhūtva yadonmukhī.
Parākularasonmādamodinī ca vikāriṇi.

At this second stage Brahma, Hari, Śaṁbhu appear and with them the Worlds (Loka) and the Elements (pancabhūtāni) of which they are composed. By the differentiation of Śiva and Śakti the Guṇas commence to operate (Śivaśaktiprabhedena guṇotpattistu jāyate—शिवशक्तिप्रभेदेन गुणोत्पत्तिस्तु जायते). Brahma and the others are not distinct entities. They are all one and the same as parts of Her. The creation which is Mātrātmaka appears and then disappears in Praḷaya.

In the third section (vv. 24-26) the Dēvi teaches the great lesson that all scripture and ritual are unneeded where She is known; as they are unneeded, where She is not known. For scriptural teaching is a means to an end—knowledge of Her. It therefore has no use where She is known. If on the other hand religious disposition is wholly wanting these means alone will not evoke it, though they are not without their uses in educating a latent piety in the disciple. Bhairavī then says "I manifest myself as woman (that is in female form or Śakti) which is my own Self and the very essence of creation (Nārīrūpaṁ samāsthāya sṛṣtisāraṁ madātmakaṁ-नारीरूपं समास्थाय सृष्टिसारं मदात्मकम्), in order to know Thee, Bhairava, the Guru who art united with Me (Bhavayogasthaṁ-भवयोगस्थम्). She adds that even when all this is said Her Tattva is not known.

The Devi then speaks of the methods (Upāya-उपाय) of attaining liberation which is the essence of all Tantrās and is honoured by all Devatās. These means secure knowledge and awaken Tattvabodha. They destroy both merit and demerit and (v. 29) give both enjoyment and liberation Bhogamuktipradāyakaṁ - भोगमुक्तिप्रदायकम्). This doctrine is said to have been kept as a profound secret so that it had not been divulged even to Viṣṇu, Brahmā, or Gaṇapa. It should be concealed in the heart (Gopanīyaṁ tu hṛdaye). "This wonderful secret, my child, should be kept from Paśus" (v. 40. Rahasyaṁ adbhutaṁ vatsa goptavyaṁ paśu-saṁgate-रहस्यमद्भुतं वत्स गोप्तव्यं पशुसंगते). The Devi speaking of this doctrine thus addresses Bhairava "Child (Vatsa) it strikes me with wonder and bewilders even the wise. It is replete with numerous and bewildering meanings and is the final resting place of all good disciples (Sachiṣya-paramāspadaṁ-सच्छिष्यपरमास्पदम्). It is Sadācāra according to all doctrines (Sarvavādisadācāra—सर्ववादिसदाचार) and is at the same time blamed or reprobated by all doctrines (Sarvavādivigarhita-सर्ववादिविगर्हित). It can be learnt only from a good teacher (Sadācāryaparijnaptaṁ-सदाचार्यपरिज्ञप्तम्). Follow it with care."

To begin with, the Dēvi speaks of the necessity for the acquisition of Jnānasuddhi, the purification of knowledge, and for this purpose She refers to the daily observances beginning with the morning, rites. The Sādhaka should rise in the morning, make his Praṇāma to the Kula trees (Kulavṛkṣa) and contemplate upon the Kula (Śakti) from the Mūlādhāra to the Brahmarandhra and meditate on the Guru.

The Kulavṛkṣas according to the Kāmeśvara-Tantra are Śleṣmātaka, Karanja, Niṁba, Aśvattha, Kadaṁba, Bilva, Vaṭa, Aśoka.

2

श्लेष्मातककरञ्जाश्च निम्बाश्वत्थकदम्बकाः ।
बिल्वो वटोऽप्यशोकश्च इत्यादौ कुलपादपाः ॥

Sleşmātakakaranjāśca nimbāśvatthakadambakah.
Bilvo vatospyaśokaśca ityādau kulapādapāh.

The Tārā-rahasya-vārttika quoting the above verse from the Kāmesvara-Tantra adds that the above are those usually enumerated but that a ninth is added by some namely the Cincā. The printed Tantra-sāra however gives a list of ten trees *viz.*, the first seven mentioned together with Udumbara, Dhātrī and Cincā.

श्लेष्मातककरञ्जाश्च विल्वाश्वत्थकदम्बकाः ।
निम्बो वटोदुम्बरश्च धात्री चिञ्चा दश स्मृताः ॥

Sleşmātakakarancāśca bilvāśvatthakadambakāh.
Nimbo vatōdumbarāśca dhātri cincā daśa smrtāh.

From which it would appear that whilst Sleşmātaka, Karanja, Bilva, Aśvattha, Kadamba, Nimba and Vaṭa are generally recognised as Kula trees, Udumbara, Dhātrī, Cincā, and Aśoka are only exceptionally so. Then follows the mental worship of the eight Kulanāthās, namely Prahlādānanda, Sanakānanda, Kumārānanda, Vasiṣṭānanda, Krōdhānanda, Śukhānanda, Jnānānanda and Bodhānanda. Their Dhyāna is given in two verses. They are those whose eyes betray the bliss in their hearts which comes from the great Rasa. "Mahārasarasollāsahṛdayānandalocanaḥ-महारसरसोल्लासहृदयानन्दलोचनः" whose darkness (Tamas) has been cut and crushed by embracing Kula; the dispellers of fear who know the meaning of all the Kula-Tantras (I. 36-37). The Chapter closes with the instruction that the Guru fit to initiate a disciple in this system must be a Kulīna and no other. The Kulīna is Adhikārī of all Vidyās and is competent to initiate in all Mantras (Dikṣaprabhuḥ sa evatra sarva-mantrasya nāparaḥ.—दीक्षाप्रभुः स एवात्र सर्वमन्त्रस्य नापरः) The work of those who leave the Kulaguru is stated to be mere Abhicāra.

CHAPTER II

This chapter begins with the ablution-riters (Snāna) and states the Śāstric rules which must be followed. The devotee, after ablution, is directed to wear two pieces of cloth (II. 12). This is strictly in accordance with the rules laid down by Yoga-Yājnavalkya. A departure from this rule constitutes, according to Bhṛgu, nakedness, which disqualifies for the performance of religious rites. The devottee is next directed to worship Śakti with offerings of flowers, incense, perfumed betel and other desirable articles. Then follows the worship with Yantra and the contemplation of Oneness with the Mother. The worship of the Sādhakā's wife Nijakāntaṁ-निजकान्तम् (II. 30) is described with the details of her initiation to be given where She has previously been uninitiated.

CHAPTER III

The rites prescribed for the night are disclosed in this Chapter. If the devotee worships Parāśakti, he should first initiate her if she happens to be uninitiated. The mantra for such initiation is referred to in three verses (III. 13-15). The food to be offered to Śakti during the Puraścaraṇa-ceremony is enumerated at length (III. 22-26). The Śaktis worshipped are to be looked upon as eight Mātṛkās and they should be named accordingly. The hymn to be recited in their worship is given, which shows that each of them is to be addressed as one of the aspects of the Mother Herself.

The hymn is called Karṇejapa-stotra from the fact that each verse addressed to each of the Mātṛkās is whispered into her ear. In this worship the elder may bow down to the younger, one of superior caste to one of inferior caste, for the Śaktis selected for worship are each and all manifestations of the Mother. The following translation and accompanying notes are by the General Editor.

OṀ

1.

Oṁ Mātar dēvi Namastēṣstu Brahmarūpadharēsnaghe.[1]
Kṛpayā hara vighnaṁ mē mama siddhiṁ prayaccha mē.

Obeisance to Thee O Mother! O Devi!
The pure One Who art Brahma
Remove by Thy mercy all obstacles which beset me
And grant me liberation.

1. Brahmarûpadhare e, sakti of Brahmâ or Brâhmî sakti.

2.

Māhēśi Varadē Devi Paramānandarūpiṇi.[1]
Kṛpayā ....

Our great Lady! Bestower of blessings!
Oh Devi! Who art the Supreme Bliss
Remove by Thy mercy all obstacles which beset me
And grant me liberation.

3.

Kaumāri Sarvavidyēśi[2] Kumāra-krīdanē varē.
Kṛpayā ....

Kaumārī! beautiful Playmate of Kumāra!
The sovereign Mistress of all Vidyās!
Remove by Thy mercy all obstacles which beset me
And grant me liberation.

4.

Viṣṇurūpadarē Dēvi Vinatāsutavahini.
Kṛpayā ....

O Devī! Who borne by the son of Vinatā
Art Viṣṇu
Remove by Thy mercy all obstacles which beset me
And grant me liberation.

5.

Vārāhī[3] varadē dēvi daṁṣṭroḍhṛta-vasuṁdarē.
Kṛpayā ....

O Devī! Bestower of blessings! Who art Vārāhī
By Whom the earth was lifted on Thy tusks
Remove by Thy mercy all obstacles which beset me
And grant me liberation.

---

1. Paramānandarūpinī: for She is according to Tantra one with the Suprem Brahman Who is Bliss Itself.
2. Sarvavidyeśī; the Vidyās are various manifestations of Mahāśakti.
3. The Varāha Avatāra which succeeded the Kūrma and raised the earth from the waters in which it was submerged.

6.

Śakrarūpadharē dēvi Śakrādi-surapūjitē.
Kṛpayā ....

O Devī! Who art śakra
Who art worshipped by śakra and other Suras
Remove by Thy mercy all obstacles which beset me
And grant me liberation.

7.

Cāmuṇdē[1] mundamālāsṛk-carçitē bhayanāśini.
Kṛpayā ....

Cāmuṇdā! besmeared with blood wearing a garland of severed heads
Destructress of fear!
Remove by Thy mercy all obstacles which beset me
And grant me liberation.

8.

Mahālakṣmi Mahāmohē[2] kṣobhasaṁtāpahāriṇi.
Kṛpayā ....

Mahālakṣmī,! Mahāmohe!
Destructress of anguish and sorrow!
Remove by Thy mercy all obstacles which beset me
And grant me liberation.

9.

Pitṛ-Matṛmayē dēvi pitṛ-matṛ-bahiṣkṛtē.
Ekē bahuvidē dēvi viśvarūpē namosstu tē.

Thou art O Devī! the Father and Mother of all
And art to us in the place of Father and Mother
One Thou art yet manifold in the form of the Universe
Obeisance, Oh Devī! to Thee.

With the recitation of this hymn ends the Pūjā of the śaktis; the worship of at least one of whom is enjoined. Other rites are enumerated in the subsequent Chapters.

---

1. One of the Samhârinî manifestations of Devî.

2. Mahâmohe. As such the Mother is the Destructress of Avidyâ and therefore as the verse says destructress of all the anguish and sorrow which proceed from it.

CHAPTER IV

The devotee should be well versed in Vaiṣṇavācāra, that is, in Bhaktimārga before he can be permitted to adopt any of the special rites. He should be Udāracittaḥ (large minded) Paranindā-Sahiṣṇuḥ (patient of ill said of him) and Upakāra-rataḥ (one who does good to others). He is required to recite his Mula-mantra if he happens to come upon a deserted temple, junction of four roads and such other places which are said to be fit for worship. He is directed also to bow unnoticed to Mahākāli if he sees certain birds and animals; Grdhra (Vulture), Kṣmemaṁkari (Brahmaṇi kite), Jaṁbuki, (She-jackal), Yamadutika (raven), Kurara (osprey), Śyena (hawk, eagle or falcon), a crow and a black cat. He is further directed to do circumambulation (Pradakṣiṇa) of a corpse and the cremation ground. The Mantras to be recited on such occasions are noted. Obeisance must also be made when he sees a black flower, red cloth, a king, a prince, an elephant, a horse, a chariot, weapons of war, valorous man (Vīrapuruṣa), a buffalo, a Kaulika or an image of Mahiṣa-mardini. If he sees a jar of wine, fish or flesh, or a beautiful woman, or a Devi Bhairavi, he must bow and recite a special mantra. The Nīlā-tantra gives a fuller list of objects to which obeisance is to be made in this way. Then comes the ritual prescribed for the worship of Kāli in the cremation-ground. The Dhyāna is revealed in seven verses (IV. 39-45) As this Devi fulfils all Siddhis She is called Daksiṇākālī.

CHAPTER V

This Chapter deals with rites which are performed for the development of powers enabling the devotee to draw towards him any Deva, lower Spirits or human being he wishes. Vv. 7-8 say that if anything is taken from the subject of the rite which belongs to him or he or she are ill-treated or deceived in any way the Sādhaka is fallen (Bhraṣṭa) and dies. Harm also happens to his family from such magic (Abhicāra). The rite consists of the worship of Dakṣiṇā-kālī, The Ṛṣi of the Mantra is Bhairava and Chanda is Uṣṇik. The first Bīja is the supreme Śakti (Pūrvaṁ Bījaṁ parāśakti-पूर्वं बीजं पराशक्ति:). The Aṅganyāsa is directed to be performed with the Bīja coupled with the six long vowels. In this rite the Brāhmaṇa Sādhaka is directed to substitute for wine (where this is mentioned) honey in a vessel of copper (v. 78) or he may perform the Kula-pūjā with Kula wine.

CHAPTER VI

This part is concerned with the method of acquiring powers (Vetāla-siddhi) enabling the devotee to go anywhere he pleases. It consists in the worship of Yoga-nidrā, Kātyāyanī, Pūrṇeśī, Caṇḍī; Kāmākhyā, and Dikkara-vāsinī. The special rite of Sādhana which goes by the name of Śava-sādhana, is described in the chapter (vv. 19-28). The object of this Sādhana in this special instance is the acquisition of the power with which the Chapter deals.

CHAPTER VII

This the last chapter describes the worship of Mahiṣa-mardinī which, from the large number of stone and metal images discovered in various places, seems to have been very popular at one time. The worship of Mahiṣa-mardinī appears to have undergone gradual changes. This is indicated by the Mantra as disclosed in the Kula-cūdāmaṇi. The Mantra has been revealed in the usual Tāntrika garb by the following verse:—

त्रैलोक्यबीजभूतान्ते संबोधनपदं ततः ।
सृष्टिसंहारकौ वर्णौ विद्या महिषमर्दिनी ॥

Trailokya-bīja-bhūtānte saṁbodhana-pādaṁ tatah.
Sṛṣṭi-saṁhārakau varṇau vidya ṃahiṣa-mardinī.

This yields a mantra of nine syllables, namely; ओं महिषमर्द्दिनि स्वाहा- Oṁ Mahiṣa-mardini Svāhā. But the text (VII-5) ordains that if the Mantra and its Sādhana is disclosed at all, it may be disclosed to one who is extremely obedient to his Guru, but even then not with its Bīja. Only eight syllables should be disclosed, thus reducing the mantra to 'Mahiṣa-mardini Svāhā.

It is said that the Mantra of nine syllables should not be imparted but should in the Kali age be kept concealed, and that eight syllables alone should be disclosed with the Mantra Svāhā but never with the Mantra Namah.

It would appear from the Sāradā-tilaka, a compilation by Lakṣmaṇa-Deśika of the eleventh century A. D. that in his day the Mantra of eight syllables alone was known. The Mantra of ten syllables is not mentioned even by the Kula-cūdāmaṇi. This may be taken to suggest that the worship of Mahiṣa-mardinī is of great antiquity. Originally the mantra was of eight, nine and ten syllables. But in course of time (at the date when the Kula-cūdāmaṇi was reduced into writing, the Mantra of ten syllables had already fallen into disuse, while the Mantra of nine syllables, was discontinued. In the eleventh century A.D. (at the date of the compilation of Śāradā-tilaka) the Mantra of eight syllables only was known.

Another important change is noticeable in the Ṛṣi and Chanda of this Mantra. The Rṣi according to Rāghava's Commentary on the Śāradā-tilaka, is said to be Śāka-vatsa; the Chanda according to it is Prakṛti. The Commentator also notices that in his day according to some the Ṛṣi was also said to be Mārkaṇḍeya. But the Kula-cūdāmaṇī (VII-11.) distinctly says that the Rṣi is Nārada and the Chanda is Gāyatrī. It is noticeable that the Ṛṣi and Chanda of the Mantra for the worship of Dūrgā are Nārada and Gāyatrī. May it be that the workship of Mahiṣa-mardinī was gradually sought to be cast into the same form as the worship of Durgā? This seems highly probable from another circumstance that according to the Śāradā-tilaka-tīkā of Rāghava-Bhatta, the Pīṭha-pūjā should be performed as ordained for the worship of Durgā.

The image of Mahiṣa-mardinī is however different from that of of Durgā. Mahiṣa-mardinī according to Kula-cūdāmaṇi (VII–13) has eight hands holding on the right side, Cakra (discus) Khadga (sacrificial sword), Bāṇa (arrow), Śūla (trident), and the left side Khadga, Carma (shield).

Dhanuḥ (bow) and Tarjanī-mudrā (*vide post*). The Devī is said to be of black colour, wearing yellow cloth, and is placed on the body of a black buffalo.

This Dhyāna does not exactly correspond with the one which is noted in the Śāradā-tilaka. According to it, the Devī holds in Her hands Cakra, Śaṅkha (conch shell), Kṛpāṇa (sword), Khetaka (club), Bāṇa, Kārmuka (bow), Śūla and Tarjanī-mudrā. The Devī who is said to be of the colour of Garuḍa-stone (emerald) and bedecked with the crescent moon is described as sitting on the head of the buffalo.

In the Hymn incorporated with the text of the Kula-cūdāmaṇī (VII-33) the Devī is said to be black of colour, resembling crushed antimony and is described as holding Cakra, Dara (Śaṇkha), Kaṛtṛkā (small sword), Kheta (club), Bāṇa, Dhanuh, Triśūla and Abhaya-mudrā. So far as this Mudrā is concerned, Rāghava cites an authority to show that Tarjanī-mudrā is the same as the Abhaya-mudrā. It appears from the Tantra-sāra the Devī is to be worshipped now in this form.

The Kula-cūdāmaṇi gives no Śaṅkha, or Khetaka or Kartṛkā. It has instead two Khadgas and Carma. The Śāradā-tilaka mentions no Carma or double sword. It introduces Śaṇkha and Khetaka. The Hymn makes a further departure by changing the Khadga into Kartṛkā. This is exactly what appears to have been in vogue when the Tantra-sāra came to be compiled about 400 years ago. The Hymn therefore appears to be of a date later than this.

While the images appear to have changed in this way, the mode of worship has remained pretty fairly the same. The details are given with a view to help the reader to follow the ritual.

The worship of Mahiṣa-mardinī is in general performed in the usual Tāntrika way. The text only notices the points of difference which constitute its special features. The most noticeable of these is the Aṇganyāsa which usually embraces six Aṇgas. In the case of the worship of Mahiṣa-mardinī the text (VII-15-17) mentions only five Aṅgas. The Śāradā-tilaka (XI-25) says that in this worship Nyāsa is made only upon five Aṅgas, leaving out the Nyāsa of the eyes. The Dhyāna is given in verses 12-14. The Yantra is composed of a lotus of eight petals, in each of which (VII-18) eight Devīs are worshipped, described generally as Durgā and others (Durgādyā). Their names are given in the Śārādā-tilakā (XI-29) as Durgā, Vara-varṇinī, Āryā, Kanaka-prabhā, Kṛtikā, Abhaya-pradā, Kanyā and Surūpā. They are worshipped with the long vowels आ, ई, ऊ, ॠ, ॡ, ऐ, औ, अः-ā, ī, ū, ṛī, lī, ai, au and ah. Thus:—आं दुर्गायै नमः-Āṁ Durgāyai namah; ईं वरवर्णिन्यै नमः-Iṁ Vara-varṇinyai namah; ऊं आर्यायै नमः-ūṁ Āryāyai namah; ॠं कनकप्रभायै नमः-Ṛiṁ Kanaka-prabhāyai namah; ॡं कृत्तिकायै नमः-Liṁg Kṛtikāyai namah; ऐं अभयप्रदायै नमः-Āiṁ Abhayapradāyai namah; औं कन्यायै नमः-Auṁ Kanyāyai namah; अः सुरूपायै नमः-Ah Surūpāyai namah. The Śāradā-tilaka-tīkā of Rāghava-Bhatta says that in selecting the long vowels ṛi, lri should be rejected as neuter vowels. The Tantra-sāra, however, gives the long vowels as ā, ī, ū, ai, au, ah. The weapons are also to be worshipped along with the consonants beginning with ya or in other words the consonants beginning with ya, that is य, र, ल, व, श, ष, स, ह-ya, ra, la, va, śa, ṣa, sa, and ha are selected.

The hymn to Mahiṣa-mardinī incorporated in the Kula-cūdāmaṇī is recited by Bhairava. The text of this hymn appears to have grown defective in course of time. Reference had accordingly to be made not only to the printed edition but to Ms. copies of the Tantra-sāra in which it is quoted. One Ms. dated 1604 Śaka year found in the district of Mymensing by the travelling Pandit of the Varendra Research Society, was of great help in restoring the correct reading. The text, as printed herein may, therefore, be taken as fairly accurate. From the hymn (Vv 22-35) it appears that whilst the worship of Viṣṇu and Śiva was popular, and their votaries were applauded the Kulācāra was blamed. A translation of this hymn in English was printed in the volume entitled "Hymns to the Goddess" by A. & E. Avalon. As was there pointed out the text of the Tantra-sāra used for this translation was in parts corrupt and unintelligible and in others of doubtful meaning. A further translation with commentary has therefore been here made by A. Avalon of the text as it has now been revised: and the opportunity has been availed of to correct some errors. The following translation and accompanying notes are by the General Editor

MAHISA-MARDINI[1]-STOTRA.

1

O Caṇḍī ![2]
By Whom the act of the wicked and formidable Asura[3]
was shattered.

Do Thou wander in my heart.
Destroy my selfishness and the calamities which deeply
pierce me,
Arising from the mass of malice and fears (which assail me)
So that, free from danger,
And protected by the lotus cluster of Thy feet,
My swan-like[4] mind may swim and rejoice in the Ocean
of Bliss.

2

What fear of his enemies has he who worships Thee?
The Devas who worship Thy feet
Having abandoned the form of Nṛsiṁha [5]
Whose towering mane rivals in splendour and height
towering Mount Sumeru,

---

(1) A title of the Śakti of Śiva as the powerful victrix of demons. She is Mahiṣa-mardini. as the slayer of Mahiṣa. The Daitya Śumbha attacked Her in the form of a buffalo (Mahîṣa) ; see Caṇḍi.

(2) A form of the Devi assumed for the destruction of the Daitya Caṇḍa, and who assisted in the destrûction of the demon Raktabija ; see Markaṇḍeya-Purāṇa.

(3) Mahiṣa.

(4) Manohaṁsa ; the Haṁsa is variously described as a swan, gander, and flamingo.

(5) The Man-lion incarnation (Avatāra) of Viṣṇu, in which He destroyed the Daitya Hiraṇya-kaśipu, father of His devotee Prahlāda.

And whose fingers are outstrtched to tear (the breast of)
Hiraṇya-kaśipu[1]
Now worship (the lion)[2] *the enemy of the elephant*[3]
Server of Thy feet which destroy the bonds of the Paśu.

3

O Caṇḍī! when the syllables, the letters of which speak of Thee,
Reach the ear, then Brahmā and other Devas
Sing the truth touching Puruṣa and Prakṛti[4].
O Devī! be today gracious to me,
Devoted as I am to the kissing of Thy sacred lotus feet,
The one and only glittering abode of the essence of the nectar of all Devatās.

4

If, because of my following Your way of Kula,[5]
I suffer reproach, better is it that I shall thus be without fame.
Let me not have that which comes of the worship of
Keśava[6] *and Kauśika*[7]

---

(1) The Avatāra is generally represented with the King of the Daityas across His knees, tearing asunder with His hands and claws the latter's belly.

(2) Which accompanies the Devī as Durgā. After the destruction of Hiraṇya-kaśipu. Viṣṇu's wrath was not appeased. The world trembled fearing what He might do. The Devas asked the help of Śiva, who assumed the Śarabha form—that of a lion with wings and eight feet—who caught up Viṣṇu into the air and held him there until he had become powerless. The lion then went to the feet of Durgā, whom he accompanies.

(3) Kari the elephant form subsequently assumed by the Asura Mahiṣa. Karivairi - enemy of elephant - lion.

(4) Śiva and Śakti; the "Male" and "Female" from whose union springs the Universe.

(5) That is, Kulācāra, one of the divisions of Tāntrik worshippers, who, the verse says, are misunderstood and therefore subject of reproach: and which is contrasted in the next line but one with the more popular and conventional worship of Keśava and Kauśika.

(6) Viṣṇu. (7) Indra.

Rather, O Mother! let my heart rest in meditation on Thy lotus feet,
Worshipped by Brahmā, Hari[1], *and the Enemy of Smara*[2]
By the Eater of oblations[3] *and the Enemy of the Daitya*[4].

5

O Mother! If I be engaged in the constant contemplation of Thy lotus feet,
Then what is there which Siddhas have[5] *which I have not?*
May Thy lotus Feet be ever present to my blissful mind[6]
Thy feet from which exceeding mercy flows!
O propitious Mother! do Thou forgive me.

6

Verily and without doubt, even the Lord of Bhūtas[7] *would have perished*[8]
Maddened as He was with the joy of the embrace of (Thee Who art) His own self[9]

---

(1) Viṣṇu.

(2) Smara, the God of Love; Śiva, who slew him, is his "enemy."

(3) That is Fire.

(4) Daityāri: usually and epithet of Śri Kṛiṣṇa, but as Hari has already been mentioned, possibly the reference may be to Indra. According to Medini, Daityāri-Devatā.

(5) Siddāspada.

(6) This "mind" has a qualifying adjective viz:— "Akṣaṭasaṁpadi" of uninterrupted happiness." It is so because the Devi is dancing there.

(7) Śiva is Bhūtesvara or Bhūtanātha. Bhuta, which in a general sense means "beings," specifically refers to the Spirits by whom Śiva is surrounded, and of whom He is Master.

(8) It is by the Devī's aid that Śiva is Parameśvara, for without Śakti He is nothing, and without Her life-giving energy and suport cannot exist. As the Kubjikā-Tantra says: "Without their Śaktis the husbands are but Preta (inert corpses)." So also the Jnānārṇava; "O beloved, pure Sadāśiva, without Śakti is without motion like a corpse, for without Śakti He can do nothing."

(9) Svātmānaṁ parirabhya. Literally. having embraced Himself. The Devī is, owever, in a dualistic sense, His sacred half, and in reality one with Him and his wn self (see Mahānirvāṇa-Tantra, Chap. I) Cf. Ātmaratipriyah (Satcakra p. 64)

Had He not been freshened by the lotus fragrance of Thy feet,
Bathed in the honey which flows within
From the union of Śiva and Śakti.[1]

7

O Mother ! let the stream of heavy showers of holy devotion towards Thee
Be ever shed upon me,
Struggling and drowning[2] *alas ! as I am in the endless Ocean of Illusion*
Without taste of the water of the Bliss of Brahman
Which devotion dispels the weight of anguish from numbers of Devas.

8

May the glory of Thy feet dark as a rainlāden cloud,
Be ever in my heart
Dispelling by its lustre as of ten million suns
The darkness which overspreads my mind.
From its glittering womb were born the three Devatās,
Who create, maintain, and destroy the world,
Whose substance is pure consciousness and bliss.

9

May[3] *Devī Durgā Who gives victory and happiness*
Dispeller of fear, Victrix of fortresses and ill-fortune
Who had power to destroy the proud enemies of the Devatās,
And Who strikes terror into the hearts of thousands (of Her foes)
Ever conquer !

---

(1) Daivādvicyutacandra-candana-rasa-pragal bhya-garbha-sravat. दैवाद्विच्युत - चन्द्र -'चन्दनरस - प्रागभ्य - गर्भसवन् The meaning is not clear but Candra (moon) seems to stand for the Bīja of Śiva (which it also means) : and Candanarasa (liquid sandal flow) issues from Devi. Therefore the union of Śiva and Śakti in the Sahasrāra appears to be indicated.

(2) Mohajaladhi-vyāhāra-viddha, lit; "pierced by the mockery of the ocean of illusion."

(3) See Mārkaṇḍeya Caṇḍi Vv, 38, 39,

She it was Who, having severed the head of the Asura Mahiṣa,
Crushed and killed under Her feet him who assumed the form of a buffalo
Now bellowing, now charging, and again retreating
And from whose mouth the Asura issued.

10

In the red ocean vast and surging
Danced the great, shields weapons and streamers[1] *of the enemy*
(An ocean) clouded by the flight of discus
And the arrows of the heaving multitude of soldiers
There lay the heads of the proud and wicked Asuras
Broken and cut to pieces, tossed about by the storm of battle,
(The sight of which) sharpened the thirst and hunger of the birds of carrion.

11

I meditate (2) *upon Devī Mahiṣa-mardinī,*
Rushing in frenzy now here now there on that wonderous field of battle (for the slaughter of the enemies)
Attended by eight companion Mātṛs[3]
And on the Mantra and Vadhū Bīja[4] *in the lotus of eight petals*[5].
Within the two horns of the fierce and terrible restless and challenging head
Bent low and slanting[6] *of the maddened buffalo.*

---

(1) Cāmara.

(2) Reading Smare for vare in text.

(3) The Devī is so called vide ante the Karṇejapa-Stotra.

(4) Strīṁ the Mantra may be said with this or the Tārā (Om) Māyā (Hrīṁ) Kāma (Klīṁ) or Vāgbhava Bīja (Aiṁ).

(5) On the petals are the eight syllables Mahiṣa-mardini svahā: "Salutation to the Devī slayer of Mahiṣa"

(6) The buffalo when charging puts its head askew. The Mantra is thought of as placed between the two horns.

12

Let the Sādhaka meditate, meditate on the dark Sivā
(Mahiṣa-mardinī),
Holding in Her hands discus, lance, axe, shield, arrow,
bow, and trident,
Making the gesture[1] *which dispels fear ;*
Her mass of hair is like a bank of cloud entwined upon
Her head,
Her face most formidable awes (Her foes)
Making even the defiant falter
Her laugh is loud and terrible.

13

O Devī ! such as in this manner
Meditate upon this Thy faultless form
Or upon Thee as Durgā or other form of Thine
Worshipped by Indra and other Devas,
To them it is given to attack the cities of their foes,
And conquering their enemies, to gain a kingdom ;
They too, acquire the nectar of the knowledge of poesy,
And power to arrest, banish, and slay[2].

14

Whosoever reads or hears this Hymn
Made by me in rapt meditation upon Thy lotus feet,
Wherein is said Thy Kula worship and Mantra in hidden
form[3]
In the palms of the hands of all such
Are forthwith wealth, fulfilment of desire and liberation.
O Mother ! salutation to Thee !
May Thou couquer !

---

(1) The Abhayamudrā.

(2) Stambhanam, Uccātanam. and Māraṇam; three of the Tāntrik Satkarma.

(3) The Mantra Mahiṣa-mardini svāhā may be spelt out from the first six verses from theo fllowing words which respectively commence them. Maccitte (Ma) Hitva (Hi) Caṇdi tadviṣayāntare (Sa) Mannindā (Ma) Nirdiṣto'smi (Rdini) Svātmānaṁ and not ātmānaṁ as given in the text (Sva) and Haha (Ha).

In the concluding portion of this Chapter, the Devī says that Her chief forms are represented by Mahiṣa-mardinī, Kālī, and Tripurābhairavī, the last being considered the primary manifestation (VII-37). This work inculcates the worship of Yoginīs as a part of Kula-worship, on Kula-days (Kula-vāra) and Kula-tithis, specially on the 14th day of the moon.

[The Kula-vāras have been described in the Yāmalas from which they have been quoted in the Tantra-sāra as follows " Tuesday and Friday are Kula days while Wednesday is both Kula and Akula, the rest being all Akula "[1] Again all Tithis with an uneven number are Akula; with an even number Kula with the exception of the second, sixth and tenth which are both Kula and Akula.][2]

The evening rite, consisting in the offering of food to jackals, is described at length. The Devī towards the end says "Thou art the Guru of all the Tantras and neither I nor Hari. Therefore Thou art the Revealer of the Tantras. I entered into Thy body (as Śakti) and thereby Thou didst become the Lord (Prabhu). There is none but Myself who is the Mother to create (Kāryavibhāvinī)[3] and therefore it is when creation takes place that sonship is in Thee. Thou alone art the Father who wills what I do (Kārya-vibhāvaka) and none else.

---

(1) Ravicandrau guruh śauris cattvāraścākulā matāh.
Bhaumaśukrau kulākhyau tu budhavārah kulākulah. See Patala VII. 38.

(2) Dvitiyā daśamī ṣaṣṭhi kulākulamudāhṛitaṁ.
Viṣamāścākulah sarvāh śeṣāśca tithayah kulāh
Similarly all Nakṣatras with an even number are Kula:
Vāruṇārdrābhijinmūlam kulākulamudāhṛtaṁ
Kulāni samadhiśūnyāni śeṣhabānyakulāni ca.

(3) That is She has the disposition to act or to carry out what He wills. Shr alone has Kartṛtva for the Father as efficient cause does not act, but the Mothee in whose womb the seed of the world is sown alone does so,

मां विना जननी कापि नैव कार्यविभाविनी ।
अतः कार्ये समुत्पन्ने पुत्र त्वं त्वयि वर्तते ॥
त्वां विना जनकः कोऽपि नैव कार्यविभावकः ।
अतस्त्वमेव जनको नास्त्यन्योऽपि कथंचन ॥

Mām vinā jananī kāpi naiva kārya-vibhāvinī.
Atah kārye samutpanne putratvaṁ tvayi vartate.
Tvāṁ vinā janakah ko'pi naiva kārya-vibhāvakah.
Atastvameva janako nāstyanyo'pi kathaṁcana.

"At times Thou art the father; at others the son; at times Thou art the Guru; at others the disciple. By the union of Śiva and Śakti creation comes (Śivaśakti-samāyogāt jāyate sṛṣtikalpanā - शिवशक्तिस,मायोगाज्जयते सृष्टकल्पना). As all in this universe is both Śiva and Śakti (Śiva-śaktimaya) therefore, Oh Maheśvara! Thou art in every place and I am in every place. Thou art in all and I am in all."

RAJSHAHI
August, 1915

A. K. MAITRA.

विषयानुक्रमणिका

शिवाभ्यां नमः

कुलचूडामणितन्त्रम्

प्रथमः पटलः

श्रीभैरव उवाच—

असंख्या[1] त्रिपुरादेवी असंख्याता च कालिका ।
वागीश्वरी तथासंख्या तथा च सुकुलाकुला ॥ १ ॥
माताङ्गिनी तथा पूर्णा विमला चण्डनायिका ।
त्रिपुरैकजटा दुर्गा या चान्या कुलसुन्दरी ॥ २ ॥
वैष्णवं गाणपत्यं च महासौरमतं तथा ।
शैवं शांकरजातं च यत्किंचिद् भूतसंभवम् ॥ ३ ॥
[2]चतुःषष्टिश्च तन्त्राणि[3] मातॄणामुत्तमानि च ।
[4]महासारस्वतं चैव योगिनो जालशम्बरम् ॥ ४ ॥

---

१. असंख्या चैव

२. "चतुःषष्टिश्च तन्त्राणि मातृणामुत्तमानि च" (१-१३) इत्यतःपरं वामकेश्वरतन्त्रे "महामायाशम्बरं च" इत्युपक्रम्य चतुःषष्टितन्त्रनामान्युक्तानि । तत्रत्यपाठोऽन्तरान्तर किंचिदन्यथा दृश्यते, सोऽयं पाठो महाजनपरिगृहीततया समीचीनतया च ध्रियते व्याख्यायते च ।

"महामायाशम्बरं च योगिनो जालशम्बरम् । तत्त्वशम्बरकं चैव भैरवाष्टकमेव च ॥
अत्र पूर्वार्धे चत्वारि तन्त्राणि—महामाया (१) शम्बरम् (२) योगिनोजालम् (३) शम्बररूपाणि । शम्बरस्य द्विधोल्लेखस्तु शम्बर-बृहच्छम्बरत्वेन व्याख्येयः । कश्चित् योगिनीतन्त्रं जालशम्बरमित्येवं व्याचष्टे । तत्त्वशम्बरकमेकं भैरवाष्टकमपरमित्यपरार्धोक्ते द्वे इति षट् तन्त्राणि ।

३. तन्त्राणाम्

४. महामायाशम्बरं च

तत्त्वशम्बरकं नाम भैरवाष्टकमेव च ।
बहुरूपाष्टकं ज्ञानं यामलाष्टकमेव च ॥ ५ ॥

तन्त्रज्ञानं वासुकिं च महासंमोहनं तथा ।
महासूक्ष्मं महादेवि! वाहनं वाहनोत्तरम्[१] ॥ ६ ॥

"असिताङ्गो रुरुश्चण्डः क्रोध उन्मत्त एव च । कपालो भीषणश्चेति संहारश्चाष्ट भैरवाः॥" इत्युक्ताष्टभैरवविषयकं तन्त्रं भैरवाष्टकनाम्ना प्रसिद्धम् ।

"बहुरूपाष्टकं चैव यामलाष्टकमेव च । चन्द्रज्ञानं वासुकिं च महासंमोहनं तथा ॥"

बहुरूपाष्टक शिवदूतीसंहितानां सप्तानां मातृणामष्टौ तन्त्राणि बहुरूपतन्त्रनाम्नाभिहितानि । यामलाष्टकम्—"ब्रह्मयामलं (१) विष्णुयामलं (२) रुद्रयामलं (३) लक्ष्मीयामलं (४) उमायामलं (५) स्कन्दयामलं (६) गणेशयामलं (७) ग्रहयामलं (८) चेत्यष्टसंख्यकम् । भास्करस्तु—ग्रहयामलस्थाने जयद्रथयामलं पपाठ । चन्द्रज्ञान-वासुकि-महासंमोहनानि त्रीणि इत्यस्मिन् श्लोके ऊनविंशतितन्त्राण्युक्तानि ।

महोच्छुष्यं महादेव! वातुलं वातुलोत्तरम । हृद्भेदं तन्त्रभेदं च गुह्यतन्त्रं च कामिकम् ॥
कलावादं कलासारं तथान्यत् कुब्जिकामतम् । तन्त्रोत्तरं च वीणाख्यं त्रोतलं त्रोतलोत्तरम् ॥
पञ्चामृतं रूपभेदं भूतोड्डामरमेव च । कुलसारं कुलोड्डीशं कुलचूडामणिं तथा ॥
सर्वज्ञानोत्तरं देव! महाकालीमतं तथा । महालक्ष्मीमतं चैव सिद्धयोगेश्वरीमतम् ॥
कुरूपिकामतं देवरूपिकामतमेव च । सर्ववीरमतं चैव विमलामतमुत्तमम् ॥

अत्र पञ्चश्लोक्या अष्टाविंशति-तन्त्राणि संख्यातानि यथा—महोच्छुष्यम् (१) वातुलम् (२) वातुलोत्तरम् (३) हृद्भेदम् (४) तन्त्रभेदम् (५) गुह्यतन्त्रम् (६) कामिकम् (७) कलावादम् (८) कलासारम् (९) कुब्जिकामतम् (१०) तन्त्रोत्तरम् (११) वीणाख्यम् (वीणातन्त्रम्) (१२) त्रोतलम् (१३) त्रोतलोत्तरम् (१४) पञ्चामृतम् (१५) रूपभेदम् (१६) भूतोड्डामरम् (१७) कुलसारम् (१८) कुलोड्डीशम् (१९) कुलचूडामणिः (२०) सर्वज्ञानोत्तरम् (११) महाकालीमतम् (२२) महालक्ष्मीमतम् (२३) सिद्धयोगेश्वरीमतम् (२४) कुरूपिकामतम् (२५) देवरूपिकामतम् (२६) सर्ववीरमतम् (२७) विमलामतम् (२८) इति ।

"पूर्वपश्चिमदक्षं च उत्तरं च निरुत्तरम् । तन्त्रं वैशेषिकं ज्ञानं वीराबलि रथापरम् ॥ अरुणेशं मोहिनीशं विशुद्धेश्वरमेव च ॥" अनेन सार्धश्लोकेन एकादश-तन्त्राण्युक्तानि—

यथा—पूर्वाम्नायः (१) पश्चिमाम्नायः (२) दक्षिणाम्नायः (३) उत्तराम्नायः (४) निरुत्तरतन्त्रम् (५) वैशेषिकतन्त्रम् (६) ज्ञानार्णवतन्त्रम् (७) वीराबलितन्त्रम् (८) अरुणेशतन्त्रम् (९) मोहिनीशतन्त्रम् (१०) विशुद्धेश्वरतन्त्रम् (११) इति शक्तिप्रधानतन्त्राणां मध्ये एतानि चतुःषष्ठितन्त्राणि उत्तमानि श्रेष्ठानि ज्ञेयानीत्याकूतम् ।

१. महासांख्यं महादेवं वातुलं वातुलोत्तरम्

हृद्भेदं मातृभेदं च गुह्यतत्त्वं च कामिकम् ।
कलावादं कलासारं तथान्यत् कुब्जिकामतम् ॥ ७ ॥

मायोत्तरं च वीणाख्यं त्रोतलं त्रोतलोत्तरम् ।
पञ्चामृतं रूपभेदं भूतडामरमेव च ॥ ८ ॥

कुलसारं कुलोड्डीशं तन्त्रं विश्वात्मकं यथा ।
सर्वज्ञानात्मकं देवि! महापितृमतं तथा ॥ ९ ॥

महालक्ष्मीमतं देवि! सिद्धयोगेश्वरीमतम् ।
कुरूपिकामतं देवि! रूपिकामतमेव च ॥ १० ॥

सर्ववीरमतं देवि! विमलामतमुत्तमम् ।
पूर्वपश्चिमदक्षं च उत्तरं च निरुत्तरम् ॥ ११ ॥

तन्त्रं वैशेषिकं ज्ञानं शिवाबलिमथापरम् ।
अरुणेशं मोहनेशं विशुद्धेश्वरमेव च ॥ १२ ॥

एवमेतानि तन्त्राणि तथान्यान्यपि कोटिशः ।
श्रुत्वा देवि! न कुत्रापि जातानन्दासि भैरवि ॥ १३ ॥
तत्कथं वद सुश्रोणि! मयि त्वत्पादवर्तिनि ॥ १४ ॥

देव्युवाच—

शृणु देव! परानन्द परापरकुलात्मक ।
मन्मायामुद्रिताशेषतन्त्रज्ञानकुलार्णव ॥ १५ ॥

अहं प्रकृतिरूपा चेच्चिदानन्दपरायणा ।
क्व ब्रह्मा क्व हरिः शंभुः क्व देवः क्व मनोर्जपः ॥ १६ ॥

क्व सृष्टिः क्व स्थितिर्वापि क्व वा संहृतिभूमिका ।
क्व रागः क्व सुखं दुःखं क्व मुक्तिः क्व च साधुता ॥ १७ ॥

आस्तिक्यं क्व नु नास्तिक्यं क्व गुरुत्वं क्व शिष्यता ।
माययाच्छाद्य चात्मानं त्रिधा भूत्वा मदोन्मुखी ॥ १८ ॥

पराकुलरसोन्मादमोदिनी च विकारिणी ।
पञ्चभूतानि लिङ्गानि चैकोत्तरशतानि च ॥ १९ ॥

ब्रह्मादिभूर्भुवःस्वःस्वभावव्यक्तिरजायत ।
सर्वेऽप्याविर्भवन्त्यत्र ततो भावादिकल्पना ॥ २० ॥

शिवशक्तिप्रभेदेन गुणोत्पत्तिस्तु जायते ।
सर्वे ब्रह्मादयो यूयं मदंशा भावसंभवाः ॥ २१ ॥

परस्पराविभिन्नाश्च तन्त्रमन्त्रसमाकुलाः ।
पञ्चत्वं प्रापयित्वापि निर्वाणपदलालिताः ॥ २२ ॥

पुनराविर्भवन्त्येते प्रकृतेः परतः पुमान् ।
अहंकारः पञ्चमात्राः सत्त्वं चाथ रजस्तमः ॥ २३ ॥

एतन्मात्रात्मकं विश्वं नष्टं चाविर्भवत्यपि ।[1]
यदि मां विद्धि सर्वज्ञ! क्व चाम्नायः क्व याजनम् ॥ २४ ॥

न विद्धि मां चेत् सर्वज्ञ! क्व चाम्नायः क्व याजनम् ।
नारीरूपं समास्थाय सृष्टिसारं मदात्मकम् ॥ २५ ॥

भवन्तं भवयोगस्थं गुरुं ज्ञातुं विजृम्भिता ।
एतावतापि देवेश! मम तत्त्वं न जायते ॥ २६ ॥

देव्युवाच—

शृणु पुत्र परानन्द परिचर्याविशारद ।
योगनिर्मुक्तकानुष्ठ उपायः कथ्यते मया ॥ २७ ॥

सर्वतन्त्रैकसारं च सर्वदेवनमस्कृतम् ।
सर्वसार्वज्ञ्यदं गुह्यं तत्त्वबोधप्रबोधकम् ॥ २८ ॥

पापपुण्यैकनाशार्हं भोगमुक्तिप्रदायकम् ।
सर्वाश्चर्यमयं वत्स! विदुषामपि मोहनम् ॥ २९ ॥

नानार्थप्रसवप्राज्ञ नानार्थसंकुलाकुलम् ।
सदाचार्यपरिज्ञातं[2] सच्छिष्यपरमास्पदम् ॥ ३० ॥

सर्ववादिसदाचारं सर्ववादिविगर्हितम् ।
न मया विष्णवे प्रोक्तं न धात्रे गणपाय न ॥ ३१ ॥

---

१. एतत्तत्त्वात्मकं ज्ञात्वा ब्रह्मचारी भवत्यपि   २. ज्ञानम्

गोपनीयं तु हृदये यत्नतः परिपालय ।
एतत्तन्त्रं विना वत्स! नाधिकारोऽस्ति यद्यपि ॥ ३२ ॥

कुलाचारे तथा वत्स! ज्ञानशुद्धिं वदाम्यहम् ।
साधकः प्रातरुत्थाय कुलवृक्षं प्रणम्य च ॥ ३३ ॥

मूलादिब्रह्मरन्ध्रान्तं कुलं ध्यात्वा गुरुं स्मरेत् ।
प्रह्लादानन्दनाथाख्यं सनकानन्दमेव च ॥ ३४ ॥

कुमारानन्दनाथं च वसिष्ठानन्दनाथकम् ।
क्रोधानन्दसुखानन्दौ ज्ञानानन्दमतःपरम् ॥ ३५ ॥

बोधानन्दमथाभ्यर्च्य ध्यायेत् कुलमथोपरि ।
महारसरसोल्लासहृदयानन्दलोचनाः ॥ ३६ ॥

कुलालिङ्गनसंभिन्नचूर्णिताशेषतामसाः ।
कुलशिष्योपरिकृपापूर्णान्तःकरणोद्यताः ॥ ३७ ॥

वराभययुताशेषकुलतन्त्रार्थवेदिनः ।
एवं कुलगुरुं नत्वा विसृज्य कुलमातृकाम् ॥ ३८ ॥

कुलस्थानं समालिङ्ग्य स्नानार्थं तीर्थमाश्रयेत् ।
शाक्तं कुलगुरुं वत्स! कथितं च सुखावहम् ॥ ३९ ॥

रहस्यमद्भुतं वत्स! गोप्तव्यं पशुसंकटे ।
कुलनाथं परित्यज्य ये शाक्ताः कुलसेविनः[2] ॥ ४० ॥

तेषां दीक्षा च यागश्च अभिचाराय कल्पते ।
तस्मात् सर्वप्रयत्नेन कुलीनं गुरुमाश्रयेत् ॥ ४१ ॥

कुलीनः सर्वविद्यानामधिकारीति गीयते ।
दीक्षाप्रभुः स एवात्र सर्वमन्त्रस्य नापरः ॥ ४२ ॥

॥ इति कुलचूडामणितन्त्रे प्रथमः पटलः ॥

---

१ °कारः सुरैरपि २. परसेविनः

द्वितीयः पटलः

देव्युवाच—

अथ वक्ष्यामि ते वत्स! स्नानं कुलसुखावहम् ।
कृष्णरक्तहरिन्नीला विविधा मम मूर्तयः ॥ १ ॥

तत्र यः कुलगः शिष्यः स तद्रूपं परामृशन् ।
दिवं सर्वमथोर्वीं च पातालं भूतसंभवम् ॥ २ ॥

आचान्तः कुलदर्भेण सदर्भकुलपुष्पकम् ।
कुलपात्रे सदूर्वं च सतिलं सजलं तथा ॥ ३ ॥

गृहीत्वा कुलदेवस्य प्रीतये स्नानमाचरेत् ।
कृतसंकल्प एवादौ कुलचक्रं जले न्यसेत् ॥ ४ ॥

कुलमूलं समानीय कुलमुद्राङ्कुशेन च ।
कुलतीर्थानि तत्रैव समावाह्य कुलात्मकम् ॥ ५ ॥

तत्तोयं च त्रिधा पीत्वा त्रिधा च प्रोक्षणं तनोः ।
कुलमूलाय देवाय त्रिधार्घ्यं परिकल्प्य च ॥ ६ ॥

देवान् पितॄन् ऋषींश्चैव तर्पयेत् कुलवारिणा ।
कुलात्मकान् पुनर्ध्यात्वा कुलदेवांस्तु तोषयेत् ॥ ७ ॥

भैरवीतन्त्र एवात्र तेषां संज्ञा च विद्यते ।
भैरवाय च देवाय भैरवेण च कर्तृणा ॥ ८ ॥

भैरवाख्यं प्रदातव्यं मन्त्रमुच्चार्य पूर्वतः ।
दातृदानगृहीतं च ततो लिङ्गानुरूपतः ॥ ९ ॥

भैरवो भैरवात्मानं भावयेत्तदशेषतः[1] ।
श्राद्धे विवाहे दाने च स्नाने चाङ्गप्रपूजने ॥ १० ॥

---

१. °भावयेद्यदशेषतः

एवं चिन्तापरे देव! प्रसीदामि न संशयः ।
ततस्तृप्ता तदाशेषलोकान् प्रीणामि तत्त्वतः ॥ ११ ॥

उत्थाय कुलवस्त्रे द्वे परिधाय कुलेन च ।
तिलकं कुलरूपं च कृत्वाचम्य समाप्य च ॥ १२ ॥

कुलपीठं समारुह्य कुलदेवस्य पूजनम् ।
द्वारदेशे ततो गीतनृत्तवाद्यादितोषितः ॥ १३ ॥

कुलभूतं समुत्सार्य[2] कुलस्थानं प्रपूजयेत् ।
कुलासनं ततः क्षिप्त्वा तदभ्यर्च्य यथासुखम् ॥ १४ ॥

कुलासनं ततो बद्धा गुरुपूजाक्रमेण च ।
आत्मशुद्धिभूमिशुद्धिदेहशुद्धित्रिभेदतः[3] ॥ १५ ॥

कृत्वा चार्घ्यं ततो विद्वान् कुर्यात् कुलविचेष्टितम् ।
दीक्षिताभिः सुशीलाभिर्युवतीभिः कुलात्मभिः ॥ १६ ॥

देवतागुरुभक्ताभिः संयुतं[4] यागभूमिषु ।
नानाविधानि पुष्पाणि गन्धानि विविधानि च ॥ १७ ॥

कर्पूरजातिधूपादिवासितं पटवासितम् ।
ताम्बूलं देयद्रव्यं च धूपदीपादिकं च यत् ॥ १८ ॥

सर्वालंकारभूषाभिर्भूषितः कौलिकस्तदा ।
मूलविद्याजप्ततोयैः प्रोक्षितं स्थापयेत्ततः ॥ १९ ॥

सर्वं[1] स्वदक्षिणे स्थाप्यं वामे चार्घ्यं निवेशयेत् ।
पश्चिमे देवतायां च कुलद्रव्याणि धारयेत् ॥ २० ॥

कुण्डगोलोद्भवैर्द्रव्यैः[5] स्वयंभूकुसुमेन च ।
रोचनालाक्षयारक्तैः[6] कुङ्कुमारुणचन्दनैः ॥ २१ ॥

यन्त्रं कृत्वा तत्र पूजां कृत्वा च जपमाचरेत्[7] ।
यथाशक्ति मनुं जप्त्वा स्तुत्वा देवीं विसर्जयेत् ॥ २२ ॥

---

१. सर्व २. समुच्चार्य ३. आत्मशुद्धिं पीठशुद्धिं देहशुद्ध्यादिभेदतः ४. संचितं
५. कुसुमादिभिः ६. लाक्षया लक्तैः ७. जपमारभेत् ।

तास्ताः प्रदक्षिणीकृत्य निजा वाप्यन्ययोषितः ।
कुलामृतरसं पूर्वं[1] गुरवे विनिवेदयेत् ॥ २३ ॥

योषितस्त्ववशेषं तु स्वात्मन्येव नियोजयेत् ।
ब्रह्मरन्ध्रे गुप्तस्थाने यन्त्रलेपं तु धारयेत् ॥ २४ ॥

नास्तिकेभ्यो न मूर्खेभ्यो न पशुभ्यो न वा द्विषे।
कुलीनाय च दातव्यमथवा जलमध्यतः ॥ २५ ॥

ततः सोऽहमिति ध्यात्वा वैष्णवाचारतत्परः ।
हरिनाम्ना जातभावो भङ्ग्यन्वितविचेष्टितः ॥ २६ ॥

चोरवत् प्रविशेदेकः सदा सङ्गविलम्बितः ।
याममात्रे गते रात्रौ कुलगेहं ततः पुमान् ॥ २७ ॥

प्रसूनतूलिकामध्ये स्थित्वा कुलपरायणः ।
कुलयन्त्रं साध्यनाम्ना संकुलं कुलचक्रके ॥ २८ ॥

स्वनामाद्यङ्कितं कृत्वा कुलाचारं समाचरेत् ।
स्वशक्त्या परशक्तिं च समानयति साधकः ॥ २९ ॥

परशक्त्याकर्षणं च शृणु वत्स ! समाहितः ।
निजकान्तां समानीय सुशीलां सुयशस्विनीम् ॥ ३० ॥

कुलभक्तं गुरुं प्रार्थ्य दीक्षयेत् कुलदीक्षया ।
परानन्दरसाघूर्णलोचनां कुलजां सतीम् ॥ ३१ ॥

ताम्बूलग्रासपूरास्यो गुरुरक्षोऽभितः सुधीः ।
निजपुत्रीवदाचार्यस्तद्भालपट्टके लिखेत् ॥ ३२ ॥

शक्तिचक्रं त्रिरावृत्त्या लिखेत् कामकलां ततः ।
तन्मध्ये देयमन्त्रेण दर्भितं नामलाञ्छितम् ॥ ३३ ॥

तत्र देवीं समावाह्य ध्यात्वा देवीं प्रपूज्य च ।
ततस्तत्पुत्रिकाकर्णे ऋषिच्छन्दसमन्वितम् ॥ ३४ ॥

---

१. पूर्णं

मूलमन्त्रं त्रिरावृत्य कथयेद्वामकर्णके।
अद्य प्रभृति पुत्रि ! त्वं कुलपूजार्चने रता ॥ ३५ ॥

अ(सु)कुलाज्ञां समादाय लज्जालस्यविवर्जिता।
य[1]थोपदिष्टविधिना स मे वस्यं (श्यं) समानय॥ ३६ ॥

इत्यनुज्ञां गुरोर्लब्ध्वा प्रणमेद्दण्डवद्भुवि।
त्राहि नाथ ! कुलाचार पद्मिनीकुलनायक ॥ ३७ ॥

त्वत्पादाम्भोरुहच्छायां देहि मूर्ध्नि यशोधन ! ।
गुरवे दक्षिणां दत्त्वा ताम्बूलारुणलोचना ॥ ३८ ॥

स्वकुलं परमीकृत्य यथाभीष्टं समाचरेत्।
सा[2]ङ्गावरणपूजादौ यदि न क्षमते कुलम् ॥ ३९ ॥

तदा मूर्ध्नि गुरुं ध्यात्वा कुलामृतरसेन च[3]।
तर्पयित्वा त[4]तो देवं जपेन्मन्त्रं निराकुलम् ॥ ४० ॥

इति कुलचूडामणितन्त्रे द्वितीयः पटलः।

---

१. अथोप २. अङ्गावरण ३. तु। ४. कुलं ध्यात्वा

तृतीयः पटलः

देव्युवाच—

अथ तद्रात्रिसमये स्वकुलं तूलिकोपरि[1] ।
वामभागे समासन्नं रक्तवस्त्रविभूषितम् ॥ १ ॥
स्वर्णालंकारभूषाढ्यं रक्तगन्धविभूषितम् ।
गन्धपुष्पधूपदीपवेष्टितं सुमनोहरम् ॥ २ ॥
सर्वशृङ्गारवेषाढ्यं स्फुरच्चकितलोचनम् ।
जितामृतकुचद्वन्द्वं[2] विशालकरिकुम्भकम् ॥ ३ ॥
ललाटयन्त्रमालिख्य साध्यनामविगर्भितम् ।
तत्स्कन्धे बाहुमादाय भङ्ग्या धृतकुचावलम् ॥ ४ ॥
ताम्बूलपूरितमुखं कुलं तदभिसंहितम् ।
कूलाकुलजपं कृत्वा[3] समानयति तत्क्षणात् ॥ ५ ॥
यन्नाम्ना लिखितं यन्त्रं तमानयति तत्क्षणात् ।
शतयोजनदूरस्थां नदीपर्वतमध्यगाम् ॥ ६ ॥
द्वीपान्तरसहस्रेषु रक्षितां निगडादिभिः ।
पयोधरभरक्षुब्धमध्यमां लोललोचनाम् ॥ ७ ॥
नितम्बबिम्बविध्वस्तस्फुरज्जघनमण्डलाम् ।
साधकाकाङ्क्षिहृदयां विवरान्तःप्रसर्पिणीम् ॥ ८ ॥
कपाटलोहसंनद्धप्राकारविवरान्तरे ।
साधकान्तःसमासीनां देवतामिव चारिणीम् ॥ ९ ॥
वशयन्ति महादेव साधकस्तत्क्षणादिमाम् ।
एवमाकृष्टि सिद्धिश्चेत् साधकः कौलिको भवेत् ॥ १० ॥

---

१. भूमिकोपरि २. जितामित° ३. कुर्यात्

दीक्षिता न च योषा चेत् कथं स्यात्कुलपूजनम् ।
कुलपूजा न चेद्वत्स ! कुलमन्त्राः पराङ्मुखाः ॥ ११ ॥

अन्ययोषा यदा वत्स ! स्वयं तस्या गुरुर्भवेत् ।
वामकर्णे परां दद्यान्मन्त्रेणैनाभिषेचयेत् ॥ १२ ॥

मन्त्रं शृणु महादेव ! यथावत्कथयामि ते ।
वान्तान्ते त्रिपुरायै(तु) हृदयं परिकीर्त्तितम् ॥ १३ ॥

इमां शक्तिं पदान्ते च पवित्रं पदमुच्यते ।
ततो गुरुपदं दद्यात् मम शक्तिपदं ततः ॥ १४ ॥

कुरु स्वाहेति मन्त्रोऽयं षड्विंशत्यक्षरात्मकः ।
अनेन मनुना देव ! शक्तिशुद्धिं समाचरेत् ॥ १५ ॥

अभिषेकाद्भवेच्छुद्धी रण्डाया अतिभैरव ।
ब्राह्मणी क्षत्रिया वैश्या शूद्रा च कुलभूषणा ॥ १६ ॥

वेश्या नापितकन्या च रजकी योगिनी तथा ।
विशेषवैदग्ध्ययुता सर्वा एव कुलाङ्गनाः ॥ १७ ॥

चतुष्पथे वा नद्यां वा बिल्वमूले त्रिशूलके ।
प्रेतभूमौ बिल्वमूले हट्टे वा राजवेश्मनि ॥ १८ ॥

सिन्दूरेण लिखेद्यन्त्रं विपुलं साध्यगर्भितम् ।
तत्र संपूज्य विधिवत् कुलं कुलरसेन चै ॥ १९ ॥

तर्पयित्वा तैदन्तःस्थं पूजयेन्निशि भावतः ।
ततो लक्षप्रदानेन सिद्धिदास्ता भवन्ति हि ॥ २० ॥

पुरश्चरणकाले तु परयोषां प्रपूज्य च ।
दीक्षितां वस्त्रपुष्पाद्यैर्भोज्यैः पायससंभवैः ॥ २१ ॥

आरम्भकाले नियतं स्वयं पक्वान्नभोजनम् ।
नानाविधं पिष्टकं च नानारससमन्वितम् ॥ २२ ॥

---

१. कुलपूजा पराङ्मुखा २. तु । ३. तदन्ते च प्रजपेन्निशि चारतः

दुग्धं दधि घृतं तक्रं नवनीतं सशर्करम् ।
उपलाखण्डचूर्णं च नानाविधरसायनम् ॥ २३ ॥

नारिकेलं कपित्थं च नागरं करमर्दकम्[१] ।
निष्पावं बीजपूरं च दाडिमीफैलमेव च ॥ २४ ॥

नानारम्यफलं चैव नानागन्धविलेपनम् ।
चन्दनं मृगनाभिं च श्रीखण्डं नवपल्लवम्[३] ॥ २५ ॥

टङ्कनं लोध्रकं चैव जलजं वनजं तथा ।
नानाशैलसमुद्भूतं नानालंकारभूषितम्[४] ॥ २६ ॥

शून्यगेहे समानीय चार्घ्योदकविशोधितम् ।
अमृतीकरणं कृत्वा शक्तीरभिमुखं नयेत् ॥ २७ ॥

अष्टकन्यारूपभेदं विलोक्यामर्शचेष्टितम् ।
ब्रह्माण्याद्यष्टशक्तीनां नामभिः कृतसंज्ञकाः ॥ २८ ॥

आसनं प्रथमं दत्त्वा स्वागतं च ततः पुनः ।
अर्घ्यपानीयकं पाद्यं मधुपर्कं जलं तथा[६] ॥ २९ ॥

स्नापयेद्गन्धपुष्पाद्यैः[७] केशसंस्कारमेव च ।
धूपयित्वा ततः केशान् कौशेयं च निवेदयेत् ॥ ३० ॥

ततः स्थानान्तरे पीठमास्तीर्यं पादुकाद्वयम् ।
दत्वा तत्र समानीय नानालंकारभूषणैः ॥ ३१ ॥

भूषयित्वानुलेपैश्च गन्धमाल्ये निवेदयेत् ।
तां तां शक्तिं समावाह्य मूर्ध्नि तासां समानयेत् ॥ ३२ ॥

भोज्यं मण्डपमध्ये तु स्वर्णपात्रे सुशोभने ।
चर्व्यं चोष्यं लेह्यपेयं भोज्यं भक्ष्यं निवेदयेत् ॥ ३३ ॥

अदीक्षिताश्चेत्तास्तत्र ततो मायां निवेदयेत् ।
तासां च सव्यकर्णेषु ततः स्तोत्रं समाचरेत् ॥ ३४ ॥

---

१. नागरङ्गं सुदर्शनम् २. फलमुत्तमम् ३. सुरपादपम् ४. संमितम्
५. अर्घ्यं पाद्यं च पानीयं ६. ततः ७. पुष्पाभिः

ॐमातर्देवि! नमस्तेऽस्तु। ब्रह्मरूपधरेऽनघे।
कृपया हर विघ्नं मे मम सिद्धिं प्रयच्छ मे॥ ३५॥
माहेशि! वरदे! देवि! परमानन्दरूपिणि!।
कृपया हर विघ्नं मे मम सिद्धिं प्रयच्छ मे॥ ३६॥
कौमारि सर्वविद्येशे कुमारक्रीडने वरे!।
कृपया .... ॥ ३७॥
विष्णुरूपधरे! देवि! विनतासुतवाहनि।
कृपया .... ॥ ३८॥
वाराहि! वरदे! देवि! दंष्ट्रोद्धृतवसुंधरे!।
कृपया .... ॥ ३९॥
शक्ररूपधरे देवि! शक्रादिसुरपूजिते[1]!।
कृपया .... ॥ ४०॥
चामुण्डे! मुण्डमालासृक्चर्चिते! भयनाशिनि!
कृपया .... ॥ ४१॥
महालक्ष्मि! महामोहे क्षोभसंतापहारिणि!।
कृपया .... ॥ ४२॥
मितिमातृमये! देवि! मितिमातृबहिष्कृते।
एके बहुविधे! देवि! विश्वरूपे! नमोऽस्तु ते॥ ४३॥
एतत्स्तोत्रं पठेद्यस्तु कर्मारम्भेषु संयतः।
विदग्धां वा समालोक्य तस्य विघ्नं न जायते॥ ४४॥
कुलीनस्य द्वारदेवाः कथितास्तव पुत्रक!।
दीक्षाकाले नित्यपूजासमये नार्चयेद्यदि॥ ४५॥
तस्य पूजाफलं वत्स! नीयते यक्षराक्षसैः।

॥ इति कर्णेजपस्तोत्रम्॥

यदि व्रीडापरास्तास्तु भोजयेत्तद् गृहाद्बहिः॥ ४६॥

---

1. गणपूजिते

स्थित्वा स्तोत्रं पठेत्तावद्यावत्तृप्तिः प्रजायते ।
आचम्य मुखवासादिताम्बूलं च निवेदयेत् ॥ ४७ ॥
ततो दद्यात् पुनर्माल्यं गन्धचन्दनपङ्किलम् ।
नमस्कृत्य विसृज्यैव वरं प्राप्य सुखी भवेत् ॥ ४८ ॥
अन्या यदि न गच्छन्ति निजकन्या निजानुजा ।
अग्रजा वा मातुलानी माता वा तत्सपत्निका ॥ ४९ ॥
वयसा जातितो वापि हीना वा परमाः कलाः ।
पूज्याः कुलवरैः सर्वैर्निजाहंकारवर्जितैः ॥ ५० ॥
सर्वाभावेऽप्येकतरा पूजनीया प्रयत्नतः ।
संस्कृतासंस्कृता वापि जननी वापि निष्पतिः ॥ ५१ ॥
पूर्वाभावे परा पूज्या मदंशा योषितो यतः ।
एकश्चेत्कुलशास्त्रज्ञः पूजार्हस्तत्र भैरव ! ॥ ५२ ॥
सर्व एव सुराः पूज्या ब्रह्मविष्णुशिवादयः ।
एका चेद्युवतिस्तत्र पूजिता चावलोकिता ॥ ५३ ॥
सर्वा एव परा देव्यः पूजिताः कुलभैरव ! ।
आदावन्ते च मध्ये च लक्षपूर्तौ विशेषतः ॥ ५४ ॥
न पूजयति चेत् कान्तां तदा विघ्नैः स लिप्यते ।
पूर्वार्जितफलं नास्ति का कथा परजन्मनि ॥ ५५ ॥
तस्मात्सर्वप्रयत्नेन यदीच्छेदात्मनो हितम् ।
ममापि क्रोधसंतापशमनं विघ्ननाशनम् ॥ ५६ ॥
यत्नतः पूजनीयाः स्युः कुलाकुलजनाः स्वतः ।
प्रातरुत्थाय पूजायां स्नानकालेऽथवा पुनः ॥ ५७ ॥
संस्कृतासंस्कृता वापि हीनजातापि वा सुत ! ।
नमस्याः सर्वजातीनां कुलीनानां कुलार्चने ॥ ५८ ॥
पुरश्चरणकालेऽपि यदि स्यात्पीठदर्शनम् ।
तदा तत्र पीठपूजा मनसापि न हीयते ॥ ५९ ॥

---

१. विसृज्य प्रदक्षिणीकृत्य २. वासंख्या ३. सत्यब्रह्मसुरादयः ।

देवीकूटे महाभागामुड्डीयाने च भैरव ! ।
योगनिद्रां कामरूपे महिषासुरमर्दिनीम् ॥ ६० ॥

कात्यायनीं कामभूमौ कामाख्यां कामदायिनीम् ।
जालंधरे च पूर्णेशीं पूर्णशैले च चण्डिकाम् ॥ ६१ ॥

कामरूपां तु ठेहारे पूज्या दिक्करवासिनी ।
अथवा कामरूपस्य दर्शनं यदि भाग्यतः ॥ ६२ ॥

तदा दुर्गादिदेवीनां पूजा तत्र विधीयते ।
कुलनाथं ततो ध्यात्वा स्वयमव्यग्रमानसः ॥ ६३ ॥

शेषं समापयेद्वत्स ! तदनुस्मृतिपूर्वकम् ।
पूजाकाले हीनजाता स्वयोषिद्वा प्रयत्नतः ॥ ६४ ॥

पूजनीया प्रयत्नेन द्वैधं तत्र विवर्जयेत् ।
यथा विष्णुः परं गोप्ता यथा च शंभुरीश्वरः ॥ ६५ ॥

यथा कमलजन्मापि ये वा व्याससुखा द्विजाः ।
इन्द्राद्या लोकपालाश्च सर्वे गन्धर्वकिंनराः ॥ ६६ ॥

यक्षरक्षःपिशाचाद्या गुह्यचारणखेचराः ।
तैर्यथा गोपितं गुह्यं त्वदुक्तं शास्त्रसंभवम् ॥ ६७ ॥

तथा त्वयैव गोप्तव्यः कुलाचारः सुदुर्लभः ॥ ६८ ॥

इति कुलचूडामणितन्त्रे तृतीयः पटलः ।

---

१. भगादि

चतुर्थः पटलः

देव्युवाच—

शृणु पुत्र ! रहस्यं मे समयाचारसंभवम् ।
येन हीना न सिद्ध्यन्ति [1]जन्मकोटिशतैरपि ॥ १ ॥

मानवः कुलशास्त्राणां कुलचर्यानुचारिणाम् ।
उदारचित्तः सर्वत्र वैष्णवाचारतत्परः ॥ २ ॥

परनिन्दासहिष्णुः स्यादुपकाररतः सदा ।
[2]देवतायतने चैव निर्जने शून्यमण्डपे ॥ ३ ॥

चतुष्पथे जले मध्ये यदि दैवाद्गतिर्भवेत् ।
क्षणं ध्यात्वा मनुं जप्त्वा नत्वा गच्छेद्यथासुखम् ॥ ४ ॥

गृध्रं वीक्ष्य महाकालीं नमस्कुर्यादलक्षितः ।
क्षेमंकरीं तथा वीक्ष्य जम्बुकीं यमदूतिकाम् ॥ ५ ॥

कुररं श्येनकाकौ तु कृष्णमार्जारमेव च ।
पूर्णोदरि ! महाचण्डे ! मुक्तकेशि ! बलिप्रिये ! ॥ ६ ॥

कुलाचारप्रसन्नास्ये ! नमस्ते शंकरप्रिये !
श्मशानं च शवं दृष्ट्वा प्रदक्षिणमनुव्रजन् ॥ ७ ॥

प्रणम्यानेन मन्त्रेण मन्त्री सुखमवाप्नुयात् ।
घोरदंष्ट्रे ! कठोराक्षि ! किटिशब्दप्रणादिनि ! ॥ ८ ॥

[3]घोरघोररवे मातर्नमस्ते चितिवासिनि ! ।
[4]कृष्णपुष्पं रक्तवस्त्रं विलोक्य त्रिपुरात्मिकाम् ॥ ९ ॥

[5]प्रणमेद्दण्डवद्भूमाविमं [6]मन्त्रमुदीरयन् ।
बन्धूकपुष्पसंकाशे ! त्रिपुरे ! भयनाशिनि ! ॥ १० ॥

---

१. कुला: कोटिसहस्रशः २. पर्वते विपिने ३. घोर घोररवास्फाले ४. रक्त-वस्त्रां रक्तपुष्पां ५. प्रणम्य ६. स्तोत्र°

भाग्योदयसमुत्पन्ने ! नमस्ते वरवर्णिनि ! ।
कृ[1]ष्णवर्णं तथा पुष्पं राजानं राजपुत्रकम् ॥ ११ ॥
हस्त्यश्वरथशस्त्राणि फ[2]लकं वीरपूरुषम् ।
महिषं कुलदेवं च दृष्ट्वा महिषमर्दिनीम् ॥ १२ ॥
प्रणम्य जयदुर्गां वा स च विघ्नैर्न लिप्यते ।
जय देवि ! जगद्धात्रि ! [3]त्रिपुरेऽम्बे त्रिदेवते ! ।
मद्यभाण्डं समालोक्य मत्स्यं मांसं वरस्त्रियम् ॥ १४ ॥
दृष्ट्वा च भैरवीं देवीं प्रणम्य [4]विमृशेन्मनुम् ।
घोरविघ्नविनाशाय कुलाचारसमृद्धये ॥ १५ ॥
नमामि वरदे देवि ! मुण्डमालाविभूषिते ! ।
रक्तधारासमाकीर्णवदने ! त्वां नमाम्यहम् ॥ १६ ॥
सर्वविघ्नहरे देवि ! नमस्ते हरवल्लभे ।
एतेषां दर्शने वत्स ! यदि [5]नैवं प्रकुर्वते ।
शक्तिमन्त्रं पुरस्कृत्य तस्य सिद्धिर्न जायते ॥ १७ ॥
एतेषां मारणोच्चाटं हिंसनं वागुरादिभिः ।
क्रियते यदि पापात्मा मद्भक्तः स कथं भवेत् ॥ १८ ॥
प्रधानांशसमुद्भूता एते कुलजनप्रि[6]याः ।
डाकिन्यश्च तथा सर्वा मदंशाः शृणु भैरव ! ॥ १९ ॥
लब्धसिद्धिसमायोगात् डा[7]किनीहिंसनं यदि ।
अथ वा दानवानां च मद्भक्तानां विशेषतः ।
वटुकानां भैरवाणां तस्य सिद्धिर्न जायते ॥ २० ॥
ग्रामे वा नगरे वाथ हट्टे वा चत्वरेऽपि वा ।
यं दृष्ट्वा युवतिर्नारी पूर्वदोषविवर्जिता ॥ २१ ॥
भावैकभिन्नहृदया वक्रदृष्ट्या विलोक्य च ।
दृष्ट्वा मधुकरश्रेणी यथा मधुमदाकुला ॥ २२ ॥

---

१. कृष्णवस्त्रां कृष्णपुष्पां २. फलकान् वीरपुरुषान् ३. महिषघ्नि नमोऽस्तु ते ४. विमृशन् ५. वैरं ६. जनाश्रयाः ७. डाकिन्या हिंसनं

पतत्यविरतं पद्मे यथा वामृतलोलुपा ।
चकोरी मेघमासाद्य सोत्सुका चातकप्रिया ॥ २३ ॥
नवप्रसूता धेनुर्वा यथा वत्सानुसङ्गिनी ।
नवेन तृणजातेन यथा वा हरिणाङ्गना ॥ २४ ॥
क्रव्यादाः पलमासाद्य तृष्णार्तास्तोयदर्शनात् ।
मृणालदर्शना हंसी मधुलोभात्पिपीलिका ॥ २५ ॥
चञ्चला निजवंशा चेद् भावना मूढमानसा[1] ।
उत्क्षिप्य भुजमूलं[2] च वसनं क्षिप्यते पुनः ॥ २६ ॥
चेलाञ्चलपरीवर्तदर्शितापघनाकुला ।
कण्डूतिभावव्याजेन शिथिलीकृतवाससी ॥ २७॥
दर्शितस्तनपर्यन्तभूभागा[3] पुनरावृता ।
स्खलत्पदयुगापातपतिता पुनरुत्थिता ॥ २८ ॥
सखीमिव्याजमासाद्य कर्णाकर्णिमनोहरम् ।
एतत्प्रणययोगेन रहस्ये कामकल्पना ॥ २९ ॥
लेखेयं पश्य सुश्रोणि शशाङ्कस्य कुचोपरि ।
इत्यादिभावभरितघृणालज्जाविवर्जिता ॥ ३० ॥
कामासहिष्णुहृदया दूरे वा चान्तिके स्थिता ।
दूतीमुखेन लेखैर्वा जिज्ञासास्फुरिताधरा ॥ ३१ ॥
कस्त्वं कस्यासि पुत्रो वा कस्मादागत एव वा ।
किमर्थं किमनुष्ठाता किं वा तेऽभिमतं वद ॥ ३२ ॥
अङ्गुष्ठकेशपर्यन्तं पीत्वापि च न शाम्यति ।
तदा तद्भावचतुरो भावबोधहविर्भुजे ॥ ३३ ॥
तस्यां निजमनोहारि हविःशेषं विधाय च ।
तत्र स्थित्वा पुरःक्षोभं कुर्यात् काम इवापरः ॥ ३४ ॥
भौमवारे चितास्थाने कुलसिन्दूरमानयेत् ।
तेनैव कुलकाष्ठेन यन्त्रं कृत्वा तदन्तरे ॥ ३५ ॥

---

१. गूढ २. मूलस्य ३. भागा वा

स्फें[1] स्फें किटिकिटिद्वन्द्वं लिखेच्चण्डमनुं ततः ।
पत्रे महिषमर्दिन्या नववर्णं लिखेत्ततः ॥ ३६ ॥

तद्बाह्ये जयदुर्गाख्यां श्मशानभैरवीं ततः ।
लिखित्वा पूजयेद्रात्रौ भद्रकालीं समाहितः ॥ ३७ ॥

कामाख्यां [2]दिशमास्थाय ध्यात्वा कामकलां तनुम् ।
दिग्वासा गलिताशेषचिकुरः कुलकौलिकः ॥ ३८ ॥

ध्यायेत् कालीं करालास्यां दंष्ट्रालीनविलोचनाम् ।
स्फुरच्छवकरश्रेणीकृतकाञ्चीं दिगम्बरीम् ॥ ३९ ॥

वीरासनसमासीनां महाकालोपरिस्थिताम् ।[3]
श्रुतिमूलसमाकीर्णसृक्कनीं चण्डनादिनीम् ॥ ४० ॥

मुण्डमालागलद्रक्तचर्चितां पीवरस्तनीम् ।
मदिरामोदितास्फे[4]फालकम्पिताखिलमेदिनीम् ॥ ४१ ॥

वामे खड्गं खण्डमुण्डधारिणीं दक्षिणे करे ।
वराभययुतां घोरवदनां लोलजिह्विकाम् ॥ ४२ ॥

शकुन्तपक्षसंयुक्तवामकर्णविभूषणाम् ।
शिवाभिर्घोररावाभिः सेवितां प्रलयोदिताम्[5] ॥ ४३ ॥

चण्डहासचण्डनादचण्डास्फालैश्च भैरवैः ।
गृहीतनरकङ्कालैर्जयशब्दपरायणैः ॥ ४४ ॥

सेविताखिलसिद्धौघसेविभिः सेवितां पराम् ।
एवं तां कालिकां ध्यात्वा पूजयेत् कुलसिद्धये[6] ॥ ४५ ॥

विना परपुरावेशविवरान्तःप्रवेशनम् ।
यत् किञ्चित् कुलसिद्धिस्तु जायते न मनागपि ॥ ४६ ॥

सर्वसिद्धिप्रदा देवी हेलयापि च चिन्तिता ।
अतः सा दक्षिणा नाम्नी त्रिषु लोकेषु गीयते ॥ ४७ ॥

---

१. स्फ्रें स्फ्रें २. देश ३. ०पवेष्टिताम् ४. स्फार ५. प्रणवोदिताम्
६. नायकः

ततोऽष्टशतमामन्त्र्य सिद्ध्यर्थं श्वेतसंभवम् ।
कालीमन्त्रेण साध्यादिग्रथितेन च भैरव ! ॥ ४८ ॥

विसृज्य देवीं हृदये स्थापयित्वा चतुष्पथे ।
वरालंकाररचितो विशेत् परपुरं ततः ॥ ४९ ॥

देवीं ध्यात्वा द्वारदेशे नमस्कृत्य कुलं गुरुम् ।
सिद्धार्थं वामहस्ते तु गृहीत्वा मन्त्रमुच्चरन् ॥ ५० ॥

यत्र च द्वारि निगडलौहशङ्कुकुलावृतिः ।
भित्त्वा तत्र विशेद्रात्रौ निःशङ्कः क्षोभवर्जितः ॥ ५१ ॥

शतावृतिं समुल्लंघ्य विहरेत् स्वेच्छया ततः ।
अश्वागारे रथागारे कालिकागारसंनिधौ ॥ ५२ ॥

देवतायतने वापि अञ्जनाञ्चितलोचनः ।
ध्यात्वा स्वप्नवतीं त्रियां[1] प्रविशेत् कामभण्डपम् ॥ ५३ ॥

यदि कोऽपि समायाति न भयं तत्र चिन्तयेत् ।
के यूयमिति वक्तव्ये वयं च वीरपूरुषाः ॥ ५४ ॥

वक्तुं ग्रहीतुं स्मर्तुं वा न शक्ताः पुरपालकाः ।
तत्र प्रदक्षिणीकृत्य पितरौ परमास्पदम् ॥ ५५ ॥

पूजयेद्यन्त्रमालिख्य निजं मन्त्रं जपेत्ततः ।
देवीकूटे तथोड्डीने कामरूपे ततस्तटे ॥ ५६ ॥

जालंधरे ततः पूर्णे यज्ञभूमौ ततः परम् ।
एषु विन्यस्य चक्राणि पूजयित्वा प्रणम्य च ॥ ५७ ॥

अष्टधा दशधा वापि शतं वापि सहस्रकम् ।
जप्त्वा पीठं समादाय भाण्डागारं ततो विशेत् ॥ ५८ ॥

निर्मूलां भूमिमास्थाय तत्र सिद्धासनं ततः ।
रक्षापीठं पुरस्कृत्य प्रणमेत् पीठसंमुखम् ॥ ५९ ॥

आगतासि महाभागे ! सिद्धयोने ! मदिष्टदे ! ।
कुलपूजां करिष्यामि उपचारं प्रयच्छ मे ॥ ६० ॥

---

१. देवीं

पुत्राज्ञां मस्तके कृत्वा ततः सागारमीक्षते ।
कुलपुष्पं[1] तथा गन्धं नैवेद्यं पुनराहरेत् ॥ ६१ ॥
तद्धस्तावचितं सर्वं तेनैवोपस्कृतं ततः ।
समादाय तथा पूजां कृत्वा पक्त्वा निजेच्छया ॥ ६२ ॥
शालितण्डुलमादाय मत्स्यमांसानि चैव हि ।
घृतं मधु तथा चान्यद् यद्वा यत्रैव लभ्यते ॥ ६३ ॥
स्थापयित्वा ततः पात्रे परमीकृत्य साधकः ।
निजेष्टदेवतां ध्यात्वा निवेद्य शास्त्रमार्गतः ॥ ६४ ॥
फलं छित्वा द्विधा भित्वा तस्यार्धं कुलशक्तये ।
निवेदयेत् स्वयं चार्धं भक्षयित्वा पुरःस्थितः ॥ ६५ ॥
यदि नो विद्यते योषा ततस्तोये विसर्जयेत् ॥ ६६ ॥
ततः पीठं समादाय भूमिमार्जनपूर्वकम् ।
पितुः समीपे संस्थाप्य तत्त्वचिन्तापरो भवेत् ॥ ६७ ॥

॥ इति कुलचूडामणितन्त्रे चतुर्थः पटलः ॥

---

१. फलं पुष्पं

पञ्चमः पटलः

श्रीदेव्युवाच—

निद्रावशगते देव ! निशाचारेण साधकः ।
कामरूपं प्रविश्याशु कामाख्यायोनिमण्डपम् ॥ १ ॥

[1]परिष्कृत्य कुलैर्द्रव्यैर्लिखित्वा चक्रमुत्तमम् ।
साध्यसाधकनाम्ना च दर्भितं विपुलीकृतम् ॥ २ ॥

कामस्थं काममध्यस्थं कामेन च पुटीकृतम् ।
कामेन कामयेत् कामं कामं [2]कामेन योजयेत् ॥ ३ ॥

ततो ध्यात्वा मनुं जप्त्वा पीठादि चावलोक्य च ।
मातृपीठे पितृमुखं स्थापयित्वा विधानतः ॥ ४ ॥

गृहीत्वा वस्त्रखण्डं वा ताम्बूलद्वयमेव वा ।
काकिणीं वा तदर्धं वा तद्योग्यं हरते हठात् ॥ ५ ॥

प्रदक्षिणक्रमेणैव क्रमेण निःसरेत्ततः ।
पौराङ्गनानां द्रव्यं वा परिरक्षितुरेव वा ॥ ६ ॥

गृहीत्वा यदि निर्याति भ्रष्टो भवति साधकः ।
तेषां प्रहारश्चातुर्यं व्यभिचारकुलक्षतिः ॥ ७ ॥

क्रियते यदि दुष्टेन तदा नश्यति निश्चितम् ।
[3]व्यभिचारात् पुरक्षोभो बद्धश्चैवाभिभूयते ॥ ८ ॥

स्वप्नप्रबोधमन्त्रेण बोधयेत् पुरवासिनीम् ।
अन्यचौरेण वा तेषां कुलीनेन च शंकर ! ॥ ९ ॥

प्रविश्य विघ्नः क्रियते साधकस्य न संशयः ।
भूताः प्रेताः पिशाचा वा राक्षसा वा सरीसृपाः ॥ १० ॥

---

१. पुरस्कृत्य २. कामी ३. अभिचारपुरक्षोभे बन्धश्चैवाभिजायते ।

किंनरी वा तथा नागकन्या पातालकन्यका: ।
विद्याधरी भैरवश्च वटुको गणपस्तथा ॥ ११ ॥

प्रविश्य विघ्नं कुर्वन्ति सुप्ता दृष्ट्वा पुराङ्गनाः ।
अपत्यहानिं विक्षोभं व्याधिमुश्चाटनं तथा ॥ १२ ॥

द्रव्यहानिं व्याकुलत्वं कुर्वन्ति विघ्नहेतुकाः ।
एतत् पुरपतेरेवं तत् कारणाद्यदि शंकर ! ॥ १३ ॥

तृणहानिर्यदा जाता तदा नश्यन्ति साधकाः ।
तस्मात् सर्वप्रयत्नेन प्रबोधं कारयेद् गुरुः ॥ १४ ॥

रक्षा कार्या प्रयत्नेन कीलकान्निखनेत्ततः ।
वज्रं शक्तिं तथा दण्डं खड्गं पाशं तथाङ्कुशम् ॥ १५ ॥

तत्र तद्दिक्पतीनां च पूजा कार्या प्रयत्नतः ।
पिष्टकं कदलं देव ! मोदकं पायसं तथा ॥ १६ ॥

भक्तं लाजं दशनं च नारिकेलफलं ततः ।
विष्णवे परमान्नं च गणेशाय च पीठकम् ॥ १७ ॥

मोदकं नारिकेलं च कदलीफलमेव च ।
क्षेत्रेशाय कृष्णच्छागं दत्वा वीरमनुं ततः ॥ १८ ॥

जप्त्वा लोष्टं समादाय क्षिपेद्दशसु दिक्षु च ।
यथा यज्ञेऽभिषिक्तेऽश्वे यथा शक्रादिभिः सुरैः ॥ १९ ॥

विघ्नमाचर्यते तद्वत् कुलोपरि महेश्वर ! ।
शयनागार ऐशाने कुलशङ्खं निधापयेत् ॥ २० ॥

ऊर्ध्वे वितस्तिविस्तारमधो विस्तारमेव च ।
कृत्वा तत्र यन्त्रराजं पूजयेन्निशि साधकः ॥ २१ ॥

रात्रौ पर्यटनं चैव रात्रौ च कुलपूजनम् ।
न करोति कथं देव ! साधकः कौलिको भवेत् ॥ २२ ॥

---

१. ०लसंज्ञकम्

गृहस्थाश्रममासाद्य प्रतिद्वारं समाहितः ।
रात्रौ स्थित्वा कुलाचारकथां त्रिभुवनेश्वरीम् ॥ २३ ॥

नैत्वा च प्रजपेन्मन्त्रं पूर्वशक्तिर्यदा भवेत् ।
प्रातः स्नात्वा गुरुं नत्वा पितॄन् देवान् ऋषींस्तथा ॥ २४ ॥

तर्पयित्वा यथाशक्ति पूजयेद्भक्तिभावितः ।
तैतो युवतिसेवाया यत्किंचिद्व्यपदेशतः ॥ २५ ॥

यथा पौराङ्गनालापमिश्रणव्यपदेशतः ।
द्रव्यादिना तत्र वापि यथा भवति भैरव ! ॥ २६ ॥

दासदासीप्रतीपालचारिणां प्रियकार्यपि ।
अस्योपरि कृपा तस्याः कीदृशी व्यपदेशतः ॥ २७ ॥

ज्ञातव्यो पुरभावस्तु यत्नतः कुलसाधकैः ।
केनापि व्यपदेशेन कुलचूडामणिं स्वतः ॥ २८ ॥

गृहीत्वा स्वर्णपात्रे वा ताम्रे वा कुलसंज्ञके ।
लिखित्वा निजयन्त्रं वा कुलयन्त्रमथापि वा ॥ २९ ॥

श्रीयन्त्रं वाथ गन्धर्वयन्त्रं वा द्रव्यमिश्रितम् ।
मध्ये तत् कुलनाम्ना च दर्भितं निजनामभिः ॥ ३० ॥

पार्श्वे कामकलाबीजं निजमन्त्रेण वेष्टितम् ।
पूजयेत् साधकश्रेष्ठः कुलाम्नायपरायणः ॥ ३१ ॥

कुलपूजादिलिङ्गैस्तु रहितो विष्णुतत्परः ।
गच्छन् स्वदन् नमन् वापि स्खलन् विष्णुपरायणः ॥ ३२ ॥

जय विष्णो हरे ! ब्रह्मन् नामाद्य पदविस्तरैः ।
स्मर्तव्योऽहं कुलाभिज्ञैररण्ये वा जलाशये ॥ ३३ ॥

ततः पूर्वोक्तरूपेण कुलक्षोभं समाचरेत् ।
ततो रात्रौ शून्यगेहे उद्याने वा सुरालये ॥ ३४ ॥

---

१. कुलाचारे २. लिखित्वा पूजयेद्यन्त्रं ३. ततः पुरपतेः ४. श्रीयन्त्रं वापि गन्धर्वदुरापं द्रव्यमाश्रितम् । ५. बाह्यतः

आनीय कुलजां देवीं मूलमन्त्रेण दीक्षयेत् ।
ततः पूर्वोक्तरूपेण कुलक्षोभं समाचरेत्[1] ॥ ३५ ॥

एवं कृतेन सिद्धिश्चेन्मूलमन्त्रं समभ्यसेत् ।
पीठानां परमं पीठं कामरूपं महाफलम् ॥ ३६ ॥

तत्र यत् क्रियते पूजा सकृद्वापि महेश्वर! ।
विहाय सर्वपीठानि तत्र[2] पुत्र वसाम्यहम् ॥ ३७ ॥

तस्माच्छतगुणं प्रोक्तं कामाख्यं योनिमण्डलम् ।
तेषां फलं महादेव! बहु किं कथ्यतेऽधुना ॥ ३८ ॥

यत्र कोटिगणैः सार्धमाद्या महिषमर्दिनी ।
यत् पीठं ब्रह्मणो वक्त्रं गुप्तं सर्वसुखावहम् ॥ ३९ ॥

यतो देवाश्च देव्यश्च ऋषयश्चैव[3] भावजाः ।
सर्वेऽप्याविर्भवन्त्यत्र तेन गुप्तं महाकुलैः[4] ॥ ४० ॥

द्विविधं चैव तत्पीठं गुह्यं व्यक्तं महेश्वर ।
व्यक्ताद् गुह्यं महापुण्यं दुरापं साधकोत्तमैः ॥ ४१ ॥

गुप्तं सर्वत्र देवेश! लभ्यते कुलसुन्दरैः ॥ ४२ ॥

भैरव उवाच—

आकर्षणविधानं मे स्वतन्त्रं समुदीरय ।
पुत्रोऽस्मि यदि देवेशि! सृष्टिसंहारकारिणि! ॥ ४३ ॥

देव्युवाच—

शृणु पुत्र! महाविद्यामाकर्षणकरीं पराम् ।
यदाराधनमात्रेण देवानाकर्षयेन्नरः[5] ॥ ४४ ॥

ब्रह्मा सरस्वतीयुक्तो देवतामुखसंयुतः ।
[6]वीरशक्तिसमाकीर्णः कालीमन्त्र उदाहृतः ॥ ४५ ॥

एकं वा द्विगुणं वापि त्रिगुणं वापि भैरव! ।
जप्त्वा कर्षयति स्वैरं स्थावरं जङ्गमादिकम् ॥ ४६ ॥

---

१. समारभेत् २. तस्या देहे ३. मुनयश्चैव ४. सदा कुलम् ५. ०येद्ध्रुवम्
६. बीजशक्तिसमाकीर्णं कालीमन्त्रमुदाहृतम् ।

एषा विद्या महाकाली गुह्याद् गुह्यतरा स्मृता ।
सुप्ता निद्रामिता मत्ता [1]भ्रामितावनता तथा ॥ ४७ ॥

समस्तदोषजालेन ग्रथिता कुलसुन्दरी ।
निशाचारं दिवाचारं संध्याचारं च पल्लवम् ॥ ४८ ॥

दर्भितं बीजसंयोगं भावयेद्योगमेव च ।
ज्ञात्वा प्रबोधयेद्धीरो गुरुस्त्रैककारणम् ॥ ४९ ॥

नियमः पुरुषे ज्ञेयो न योषित्सु कथंचन ।
यद्वा तद्वा येन केन सर्वदा सर्वतोऽपि च ॥ ५० ॥

योषितां ध्यानयोगेन सिद्धयः स्युर्न संशयः ।
यथायस्कान्तमात्रेण गूढविद्धशिलोच्चयः ॥ ५१ ॥

स्वयमेव बहिर्याति यथा वा सौरतेजसा ।
सूर्यकान्तः स्फुटरुचिर्यथा च रविरश्मिभिः ॥ ५२ ॥

चन्द्रकान्तं द्रावयति यथा वर्षासु वारिदः ।
[2]जलसेकाभितृप्ता भू रसपूर्णा प्रचक्षते ॥ ५३ ॥

पुष्पदर्शनमात्रेण भुक्तिमुक्तिर्यथा भवेत् ।
महादुर्गाप्रसादेन यथा सिद्धीश्वरो भवेत् ॥ ५४ ॥

कुलपुष्पप्रसादेन यथा प्रीतिस्तु जायते ।
गङ्गास्मरणमात्रेण निष्पापो जायते यथा ।
यथाकर्षणमात्रेण शिव एव प्रजायते ॥ ५५ ॥

योषिच्चिन्तनमात्रेण यथेयं वरदायिनी ।
तस्मात् सर्वप्रयत्नेन दीक्षयेन्निजकौलिकीम् ॥ ५६ ॥

---

१. विद्रावणरता परा ।

२. क्षुधार्तः क्षीरपानेन नरस्तृप्तोऽभिजायते ।
पुष्पदर्शनमात्रेण गन्धर्वः प्रीयते यथा ।
गुरुसेवनमात्रेण मन्त्रसिद्धिर्यथा भवेत् ।
महापद्मवनध्यानाद्यथा सिद्धेश्वरो भवेत् ।
त्रिपुराध्यातमात्रेण भुक्तिर्मुक्तिर्यथा भवेत् ।

भैरवोऽस्य ऋषिः प्रोक्त उष्णिक् छन्दस्तु देवता ।
कालिका दक्षिणा देवी चतुर्वर्गफलप्रदा ॥ ५७ ॥

पूर्वं बीजं पराशक्तिर्बीजेन मूर्तिकल्पना ।
षड्दीर्घभाजा बीजेन कुर्यादङ्गादिकल्पनाम् ॥ ५८ ॥

चतुर्दश विभागेन मातृकार्णैः पृथक् पृथक् ।
हृदये हस्तयोः पादयुगले विन्यसेत्ततः ॥ ५९ ॥

पञ्चाशन्मूलमन्त्रेण व्यापकं विन्यसेत्ततः ।
पञ्चधा ध्यानमेकत्र पूर्वोक्तं च समाचरेत् ॥ ६० ॥

देशपञ्चारपद्मेषु[1] पीठपूजां समाचरेत् ।
तत्रावाह्य यजेद्देवीं दक्षिणां कुलभूषणाम् ॥ ६१ ॥

महाकालं यजेत् पश्चात् पीठशक्तिं ततो यजेत् ।
कालीं कपालिनीं कुल्लां प्रथमे च त्रिकोणके ॥ ६२ ॥

कुरुकुल्लां विरोधीं च विप्रचित्तां तथैव च ।
उग्रमुखीमुग्रप्रभां प्रदीप्तां च तथैव च ॥ ६३ ॥

नीलां घनां बलाकां च सितां धात्रीं च मुद्रिकाम् ।
ब्रह्माण्याद्यास्तथा बाह्ये यजेत् पूर्वदले क्रमात् ॥ ६४ ॥

एवं कृत्वा जपेन्मन्त्रं हविष्याशी दिवा शुचिः ।
लक्षं रात्रौ तथा लक्षं महाशौचपरायणः ॥ ६५ ॥

अन्यासां योषितां चात्र न पूजा नापि चिन्तनम् ।
रात्रौ जपैकमात्रेण सिद्धिदा दक्षिणा भवेत् ॥ ६६ ॥

अङ्गन्यासं समाचर्य ध्यात्वा देवीं जपेद् बुधः ।
अरण्यामथवा रात्रौ महाकाली महोदया ॥ ६७ ॥

अनेनैव विधानेन पूजिता विश्वरूपिणी ।
आकर्षयेद्देवकन्यां पाताले नागकन्यकाम् ॥ ६८ ॥

---

१. दशधा योगपद्मेषु

अरण्या च महाकाली द्वितीया चेयमीरिता ।
पूजा ध्यानं प्रयोगं च जपं चैव विशेषतः ॥ ६९ ॥

समानं सर्वमेतस्यास्तस्या देव्याः प्रकीर्त्तितम् ।
जपादिकं वारि सर्वं पूर्वोक्तं चात्र कीर्तितम् ॥ ७० ॥

अरण्या च महाकाली पूजायां निर्मला भवेत् ।
ईशाने शङ्खमासाद्य तत्र यन्त्रं विलिख्य च ॥ ७१ ॥

अष्टमीरात्रिमारभ्य चतुर्दश्यां समापयेत् ।
अष्टोत्तरशतं मर्त्यो मन्त्रयित्वा सुसंयतः ॥ ७२ ॥

नग्नस्ताम्बूलपूर्णास्यो मुक्तकेशो जितेन्द्रियः ।
मदिराघूर्णनयनः परयोषित्समागमे ॥ ७३ ॥

पूजयेद् गन्धपुष्पेन दिग्वासाः कुलभूषणः ।
यन्नाम्ना दर्भितं यन्त्रं पूजयेद्वीरवल्लभः ॥ ७४ ॥

सा समायाति कामार्ता यत्र देशे स पूजकः ।
मद्यं मांसं तथा वत्स ! यत् किंचित् कुलसाधनम् ॥ ७५ ॥

तस्यै दत्त्वा ततः शेषं गुरवे विनिवेद्य च ।
तदनुज्ञां मूर्ध्नि कृत्वा शेषं चात्मनि योजयेत् ॥ ७६ ॥

मद्यं मांसं विना वत्स ! कुलपूजां समाचरेत् ।
जन्मान्तरसहस्रस्य सुकृतं तस्य नश्यति ॥ ७७ ॥

यत्रावश्यं विनिर्दिष्टं मदिरादानपूजनम् ।
ब्राह्मणस्ताम्रपात्रेषु मधु मद्यं प्रकल्पयेत् ॥ ७८ ॥

अथवा कुलमद्येन पूजयेत् कुलपूजितम् ।
योगिभिः पीयते मद्यं तन्मद्यं योगिपुंगवैः ॥ ७९ ॥

न मद्यं पानयोग्यं स्याद्यन्मद्यं गुडपिष्टकम् ॥ ८० ॥

इति कुलचुडामणितन्त्रे पञ्चमः पटलः ।

षष्ठः पटलः

देव्युवाच—

अथ वक्ष्यामि ते वत्स! विधानं यत्र यद् भवेत् ।
आनीय देवीं तद् गात्रे व्यापकं विन्यसेत्ततः ॥ १ ॥

प्रथमं साधकश्रेष्ठो देवीकूटस्य मस्तके ।
विलिख्य यन्त्रं पूर्वोक्तं पूजयेत कुलवर्त्मना ॥ २ ॥

पीठादि देवीं प्रणमेत् पूजयेद् गन्धपुष्पकैः ।
महाभागां ततो मूलदेवीमावरणैः सह ॥ ३ ॥

लक्षैकं तत्र जप्त्वा तु उड्डीयानं ततो विशेत् ।
तत्पीठे योगनिद्राख्यां पूजयित्वा ततो यजेत् ॥ ४ ॥

निजेष्टदेवतां तत्र जपेल्लक्षं समाहितः ।
कामरूपं ततो गत्वा ततः कात्यायनीं यजेत् ॥ ५ ॥

जप्त्वा लक्षं ततो रात्रौ कामाख्यां प्रथमं यजेत् ।
ततो जालंधरे गत्वा पूर्णेशीं प्रथमं यजेत् ॥ ६ ॥

तत्रापि लक्षमानेन जप्त्वा मन्त्रं समाहितः ।
ततः पूर्णगिरौ गत्वा यजेच्चण्डीं ततो जपेत् ॥ ७ ॥

कामरूपान्तरे गत्वा कामाख्यां प्रथमं यजेत् ।
ततः प्रान्ते महादेवीं यजेद्दिक्करवासिनीम् ॥ ८ ॥

एवं पीठेश्वरीं जप्त्वा पूजयेदिष्टदेवताम् ।
सप्तपीठे सप्तलक्षं जप्त्वा रात्रौ समाहितः ॥ ९ ॥

संख्यापूर्तौ ततः पृच्छेत् का त्वं देवि! कुलोत्तमे ।
एवं कृते विस्मृता चेत् स्वनाम्नि गोत्रजन्मनि ॥ १० ॥

---

१. वत्स २. पूजयित्वेष्ट° ३. संख्या पूर्णे पुनः

तवेष्टदेवतैवाहं वृणुष्व वरमुत्तमम् ।
ततः प्रणम्य देवेशीं वृणुयाद्वरमात्मनः ॥ ११ ॥

यद्येवं नैव सा देवी पुनः पूर्वोक्तमाचरेत् ।
अक्षोभितकुलाचारपरिचर्यापरायणः ॥ १२ ॥

अथवा सर्वपीठेषु यजेन्महिषमर्दिनीम् ।
ततः प्रसन्ना भवति स्वैरं कुलवरप्रिया ॥ १३ ॥

ततो जप्त्वा मूलमन्त्रं सर्वसिद्धीश्वरो भवेत् ।
राजवृक्षं समालोक्य तन्मूले स्वेष्टदेवताम् ॥ १४ ॥

पूजयित्वा महारात्रौ त्रिदिनं प्रजपेन्मनुम् ।
लक्षपीठफलं देव! लभते साधकोत्तमः ॥ १५ ॥

वेतालं पादुकासिद्धिं खड्गसिद्धिं च भैरव! ।
अञ्जनं तिलकं गुप्तिं महिषासुरमर्दिनीम् ॥ १६ ॥

साधयेत् साधकोऽभीष्टं मूलविद्यां महेश्वर! ॥ १७ ॥

भैरव उवाच—

वेतालादिमहासिद्धिः कथं भवति चण्डिके! ।
तन्मे कथय देवेशि! यदि स्नेहोऽस्ति मां प्रति ॥ १८ ॥

देव्युवाच—

[२]निम्बवृक्षोद्भवं काष्ठं श्मशाने साधकोत्तमः ।
भौमवारे मध्यरात्रौ शवासनयुगाङ्किते ॥ १९ ॥

खनित्वा चाष्टलक्षं वै जपेन्महिषमर्दिनीम् ।
तत्सहस्रं हुनेद्वत्स! तत्रैव पितृकानने ॥ २० ॥

काष्ठमुद्धृत्य तत्रैव दण्डेपादुकचिह्नितम् ।
गत्वा दुर्गाष्टमीरात्रौ श्मशाने निक्षिपेत्ततः ॥ २१ ॥

तस्योपरि शवं कृत्वा पूजयित्वा यथाविधि ।
शवासनगतो वीरो जपेदष्टसहस्रकम् ॥ २२ ॥

---

१. तत्त्वं २. बिल्व

ततो मातृबलिं दत्त्वा काष्ठमामन्त्रयेत्ततः ।
[1]स्फें स्फें दण्ड महाभाग योगिनीहृदयप्रिय! ॥ २३ ॥

मम हस्तस्थितो नाथ! ममाज्ञां परिपालय ।
एवमामन्त्र्य वेतालं यत्र यत्र प्रयुज्यते ॥ २४ ॥

तं तं चूर्णीविधायाथ पुनरायाति कौलिकः ।
गच्छ गच्छ महाभागे! पादुके! वरवर्णिनि ॥ ॥ २५ ॥

मत्पादस्पर्शमात्रेण गच्छ त्वं शतयोजनम् ।
[2]अष्टलोहं समासाद्य पञ्चाशदङ्गुलाकृतिम् ॥ २६ ॥

खड्गं कृत्वा तत्र यन्त्रं लिखित्वा[3] प्रजपेन्मनुम् ।
तत् सहस्रं ततो जप्त्वा महाशवकलेवरे ॥ २७ ॥

खनित्वा बीजवृक्षाग्रे बद्ध्वा रक्षां[4] तु कारयेत् ।
कुलाष्टम्यामर्धरात्रे चितामध्ये समाहितः ॥ २८ ॥

प्रीतिपूर्वं समामन्त्र्य हुनेत् पितृवने ततः ।
मधुरत्रयसंयुक्तं बिल्वपत्रेण संयुतम् ॥ २९ ॥

पादादिमूर्धपर्यन्तं होमान्ते बलिमाहरेत् ।
बल्यन्ते परमा माया देवी महिषमर्दिनी ॥ ३० ॥

आयाति बलिपूर्णास्या वरहस्ता मदोन्मुखी ।
गृह्ण वत्सेति शब्दे वै खड्गमुत्तोल्य धारयेत् ॥ ३१ ॥

घोरदंष्ट्रे! महाकालि! करवालस्वरूपिणि ।
कॉं ईं ॐ कुरु कल्याणि विपक्षच्छेदविस्तरम् ॥ ३२ ॥

एवमामन्त्र्य खड्गं तु यमुद्दिश्य क्षिपेन्नरः ।
छित्त्वा छित्त्वा पुनश्छित्त्वा गच्छत्याकृष्यते पुनः ॥ ३३ ॥

अथवा कृष्णमार्जारमेकघातेन छेदयेत् ।
कुजे चतुष्पथे रात्रौ निखनेन्मन्त्रितं ततः ॥ ३४ ॥

---

१. स्फें स्फें   २. खड्गबाहुं   ३. हुत्वा   ४. शुष्कं तु भावयेत् ।

तत्र मोचां समारोप्य यावत् पत्रं प्रजायते ।
तावद् भुक्त्वा हविष्यान्नं प्रतिरात्रं जपेदभीः ॥ ३५ ॥

अष्टोत्तरसहस्रं तु एकाकी दीपवर्जितः ।
उत्पन्नं पत्रमालोक्य छित्त्वा निश्छिद्रमानयेत् ॥ ३६ ॥

तत्र भुक्त्वा हविष्यान्नं तद्दिने तटिनीतटे ।
तमानीय सुहृत्सङ्गः क्षालयेन्मन्त्रमुच्चरन् ॥ ३७ ॥

तच्छ्रोतोऽभिमुखं वत्स ! यदस्थि प्रतिगच्छति ।
तदानीय यजेत्तत्र कालिकां घोरनिःस्वनाम् ॥ ३८ ॥

अभिमन्त्र्य सहस्रं तु कालीमन्त्रं समाहितः ।
सिद्धाञ्जनो भवेन्मन्त्री नात्र कार्या विचारणा ॥ ३९ ॥

चन्दनागुरुकस्तूरीमिश्रितं चास्थिघर्षणम् ।
कृत्वा [1]संपूज्य विधिवत् सर्वं जयति साधकः ॥ ४० ॥

[2]कुलमीनं कुलान्नं च कुलमद्यं कुलेश्वर ! ।
कुलस्थाने समानीय दत्त्वा देव्यै प्रयत्नतः ॥ ४१ ॥

अष्टोत्तरसहस्रं तु जप्त्वा भूमितले स्थितः ।
भूमौ फूत्कारमात्रेण विवरं तत्र जायते ॥ ४२ ॥

शतयोजनदूरे वा यत्र साध्यस्थितिर्भवेत् ।
तत्रैव गमनं तस्य भूतलान्तःप्रसर्पिणः ॥ ४३ ॥

एवं विवरमध्ये वा गवाक्षे कुहरेऽपि च ।
कायसंकोचमासाद्य गच्छत्यविकलो नरः ॥ ४४ ॥

दुर्गामन्त्रं विना वत्स ! कालीमन्त्रं तथैव च ।
सिद्धयः कुलनाथेश ! जायन्ते न कथंचन ॥ ४५ ॥

॥ इति कुलचूडामणितन्त्रे षष्ठः पटलः ॥

---

१. तिलकमादाय २. कुलमूलं कुलद्रव्यं कुलमद्यं महेश्वर.

सप्तमः पटलः

भैरव उवाच—

मातर्महिषमर्दिन्याः संकेतं कथयस्व मे ।
कुलाचारस्य संसिद्ध्यै भुक्तिमुक्तिप्रसिद्धये ॥ १ ॥

देव्युवाच—

सृष्टिस्थितिविनाशानामादिभूता महेश्वरी ।
गोप्या सर्वप्रयत्नेन शृणु तां कथयामि ते ॥ २ ॥
त्रैलोक्यबीजभूतान्ते संबोधनपदं ततः ।
सृष्टिसंहारकौ वर्णौ विद्या महिषमर्दिनी ॥ ३ ॥
अतिगुह्यतरा नित्या सृष्टिस्थितिविधायिनी ।
सर्वदेवसर्वसिद्धिबीजभूता सनातनी ॥ ४ ॥
अत्यन्तगुरुभक्ताय शुद्धाय यदि कथ्यते ।
तदाष्टवर्णं वक्तव्यं न बीजं नापि साधनम् ॥ ५ ॥
साधारणी प्राणविद्या हृल्लेखा सिद्धिगोचरा ।
एतत् पूर्वस्थिता देवी गुरुसिद्धिविनाशिनी ॥ ६ ॥
विशेषतः कलियुगे महासिद्धौघदायिनी ।
गुरूणां कुलनाथानां महाशापप्रदायिनी ॥ ७ ॥
जया दुर्गाभया प्रोक्ता परमा सिंहवाहिनी ।
त्रैलोक्यबीजभूतान्ते सा परा मर्दिनीकुलम् ॥ ८ ॥
वरं वह्निप्रिया देया[1] न देया नमसाहिता ।
दत्ता च परमा विद्या ङेयुता हृदयान्विता ॥ ९ ॥
सर्वत्र कुलशास्त्रज्ञ ! महाशापप्रदायिनी ।
तस्मात् सर्वप्रयत्नेन गोप्तव्येयं नवाक्षरी ॥ १० ॥

---

१. युक्ता

अष्टलक्षं जपेन्मन्त्रं तद्दशांशं हुनेत्ततः ।
नारदोऽस्य ऋषिः प्रोक्तश्छन्दो गायत्रमीरितम् ॥ ११ ॥
देवता महिषघ्नीयं पूर्वं वीजं परापरा ।
ध्यायेत् कालीं महादैत्ययुद्धरागमदोन्मुखीम् ॥ १२ ॥
दक्षिणे चक्रखड्गौ च बाणं शूलं तथैव च ।
वामे खड्गं तथा चर्म धनुस्तर्जनमेव च ॥ १३ ॥
बिभ्रतीं कालतीव्रोरुमहिषाङ्गनिषेदुषीम् ।
पीताम्बरधरां देवीं पीनोन्नतकुचद्वयाम् ॥ १४ ॥
जटामुकुटशोभाढ्यां पितृभूमिसुखावहाम् ।
ॐ महिषहिंसके हूं फट् हृदयाय नमो हृदि ।
ॐ महिष(दैत्य)शत्रो हूं फट् शिरस्युदीरितम् ॥ १५ ॥
ॐ महिषं हेषय हेषय हूं (फट्) शिखामन्त्रः समीरितः ॥ १६ ॥
ॐ महिषं हन हन देवी हूं फट् कवच इत्यपि ।
महिषमर्दिनी हूं फट् अस्त्राणि शृणु भैरव ॥ १७ ॥
अष्टपत्रे यजेद्देवीर्दुर्गाद्या दीर्घपूर्विकाः ।
आयुधानि पलाशाग्रे यादिभिः क्रमशो यजेत् ॥ १८ ॥
ब्रह्माण्याद्यास्ततः[1] पश्चाल्लोकपालांस्ततो बहिः ।
सिद्धमन्त्री तदस्त्राणि प्रयोगं च समाचरेत् ॥ १९ ॥
प्रयोगे होमनियमः सहस्रं वसुसंमितम् ।
एषा विद्या महाविद्या न देया यस्य कस्यचित् ॥ २० ॥
यदि भाग्यवशाल्लब्धा कुलदेवी कुलोत्तमैः ।
दीक्षिता कुलजातिस्तु सिद्धिदा सैव नान्यथा ॥ २१ ॥

महिषमर्दिनीस्तोत्रम्

भैरव उवाच—
मच्चित्ते चर चण्डि ! चूर्णितदुराचारप्रचण्डासुरे !
स्वैरं दारय भूरि दुर्धरदरद्रोहोर्मिमर्मापदः ।

---

१. ब्राह्मयाद्याश्चेति इति तन्त्रसारे

तेनायं निरुपद्रुतो निरुपमश्रीपादपद्माटवी-
प्राप्तानन्तरसार्णवे मम मनोहंसश्चिरं नन्दतु ॥ २२ ॥

हित्वा चण्डि ! हिरण्यदारणपटुप्रोद्दामहस्ताङ्गुलि-
स्फायत् कम्रसुमेरुसोदरसटाटोपं नृसिंहं सुराः ।
मातस्त्वत्पशुपाशपेषणपटुश्रीपादसंसेविनं
सेवन्ते करिवैरिणं किमरिभिर्भीतिर्भवेत्सेविनः ॥ २३ ॥

चण्डि ! त्वद्विषयान्तराक्षरपदं श्रोत्रान्तरं चेद्गतं
तत्तत्त्वं पुरुषप्रकृत्यनुगतं ब्रह्मादिभिर्गीयते ।
तस्माद्देवि ! समस्तदैवतसुधासारैकधामस्फुर-
च्छ्रीमत्पादपयोजचुम्बनपरं मामद्य संभावय ॥ २४ ॥

मन्निन्दा यदि वास्तु ते कुलपथाचाराद्वरं[1] मास्तु वा
कीर्त्तिः केशवकौशिकार्चनचरी नैवास्तु मत्संनिधिः ।
मातर्ब्रह्महरिस्मरारिहुतभुग्दैत्यारिसेवास्पद-
श्रीमत्पादपयोजचिन्तनविधौ चित्तं सदैवास्तु नः ॥ २५ ॥

निर्दिष्टोऽस्मि यदि त्वदीयपदयुक्पूर्वापरीभावने
निर्दिष्टस्य तदा ममापि विरलं किंवास्तु सिद्धास्पदम् ।
तस्माद्देवि ! कृपाभराश्चिततरं श्रीपादपद्मद्वयं
मच्चित्तेऽक्षतसंपदि प्रसरतु क्षेमंकरि ! क्षम्यताम् ॥ २६ ॥

आत्मानं[2] परिरभ्य भूतपतिरप्युन्मादमासादितः
स्फारं जीवनरक्षणे स च कृती नैवाभविष्यत्प्रभुः ।
दैवाद्विच्युतचन्द्रचन्दनरसप्रागल्भ्यगर्भस्रव-
न्माध्वीपूर्णभवत्पदैककमलामोदेन नास्वादितः ॥ २७ ॥

हा हा मातरनादिमोहजलधिव्याहारविद्धाखिल-
ब्रह्मानन्दरसाभिषेकविरसस्वान्तोदरे मादृशि ।
युष्माकं सुखवृन्दनिर्भरमनस्तापाभिभूतिक्षमः
श्रीमद्भक्तिरसातिदुर्दिनपरीवाहः सदा सर्पतु ॥ २८ ॥

---

१. द्वयं २. स्वात्मानं

यत्पादस्फुरदंशुजालजठराचण्डांशुकोटिस्फुर-
त्स्वान्तध्वान्तविसारि निर्मलचिदानन्दत्रयं दैवतम् ।
सर्गं संसृजति स्थितिं वितनुते सृष्टिं पुनर्लुम्पति
प्रोद्भिन्नाञ्जननीलनीरदमहश्चित्ते सदैवास्तु नः ॥ २९ ॥

या शश्वन्महिषच्छलस्फुटमिलद्गर्जद्द्विधावत्स्खल-
द्रक्तान्तःप्रसरत्तमस्तमशिरो दैत्यं समालम्बते ।
सा दुर्गा भयदुर्गदुर्गतिहरा लक्षान्तरत्रासिनी
दृप्यद्दैवतवैरिदारणपटुर्जीयाज्जयाह्लादिनी ॥ ३० ॥

नृत्यत्खेटकचामराश्चलवलच्चक्राद्यखर्वावर-
स्फायत्सैन्यशिलीमुखोच्छलदनल्पाजिह्मताम्राम्बुधौ ।
झञ्झावातविसर्पिनर्तितशिरःसाटोपदुष्टासुर-
त्रुटचत्खण्डविखण्डिताखिलशकुन्तक्षुत्पिपासोज्ज्वले ॥ ३१ ॥

चञ्चत्कम्रविरामकालकलतीव्रास्फालसंपादको-
न्माद्यन्माहिषतिर्यगानतशिरः शृङ्गान्तराले स्थले ।
वस्वर्णैर्वसुपत्रमध्यकलितैर्बध्वा श्रुतीर्मातृभिः
सेव्ये चारु रणाङ्गणे रणमुदा घूर्णायमानाम्बरे[2] ॥ ३२ ॥

ऊर्ध्वाधःक्रमसव्यवामकरयोश्चक्रं दरं कर्तृकां
खेटं बाणधनुस्त्रिशूलभयहृन्मुद्रां दधानां शिवाम् ।
श्यामां नीलघनोच्चकुन्तलचयप्रोन्नद्धजूटां स्खल-
द्वीरास्फाललसत्करालवदनां घोराट्टहासोद्भटाम् ॥ ३३ ॥

एवं ये तव देवि ! मूर्तिमनघां ध्यायन्ति दुर्गादिभिः
शक्राद्यैरपि पूजितां परपुरक्षोभादिकं कुर्वते ।

---

१. तत्पादस्फुरदंशुजालजठराचण्डांशुकोटिस्खलद्-
ध्वान्तस्वान्तविसारि निर्मलचिदानन्दत्रयं दैवतम् ।
सर्गं संसृजते स्थितिं वितनुते सृष्टिं पुनर्लम्पते
प्रोद्भिन्नाञ्जननीलनीरदमहच्चित्ते सदैवास्तु नः ॥

इति तन्त्रसारादृतः पाठः

२. चूर्णायमानां स्मरेत् इति तन्त्रसारे ॥

राज्यं शत्रुजयः सदर्थधिषणा काव्यामृतादर्शन-
स्तम्भोच्चाटनमारणादिकृतिनां तेषां स्वयं जायते ॥ ३४ ॥

स्तोत्रं ते चरणारविन्दयुगलध्यानात्प्रधानान्मया
मन्त्रोद्धारकुलोपचाररचितं[1] गूढोपदिष्टं यदि ।
ये शृण्वन्ति पठन्ति देवि! तरसा श्रीमोक्षकामादय-
स्तेषां हस्तगता भवन्ति जगतां मातर्नमस्ते जय ॥ ३५ ॥

देव्युवाच—

स्तोत्रश्रवणसंतुष्टा प्रीतास्मि तव भैरव ।
पश्य मूर्तिं न च ध्यानयोग्यां मम सुखावहाम् ॥ ३६ ॥

एषा मूर्तिः प्रधानं मे कालीमूर्तिस्तथैव च ।
त्रिपुरा भैरवीमूर्तिराद्या सा परिकीर्त्तिता ॥ ३७ ॥

कुलवारे कुलाष्टम्यां चतुर्दश्यां विशेषतः ।
योगिनीपूजनं तत्र प्रधानं कुलपूजनम् ॥ ३८ ॥

यथा विष्णुतिथौ विष्णुः पूजितो वाञ्छितप्रदः ।
तथा कुलतिथौ दुर्गा पूजिता वरदायिनी ॥ ३९ ॥

बिल्वमूले प्रान्तरे वा श्मशाने वापि साधकः ।
मांसप्रधानं नैवेद्यं संध्याकाले विधीयते ॥ ४० ॥

काली कालीति वक्तव्ये ततोमा शिवरूपिणी ।
पशुरूपा समायाति परिवारगणैः सह ॥ ४१ ॥

भुक्त्वा रौति यदैशान्यां मुखमुत्तोल्य सुस्वरम् ।
तदैव मङ्गलं तस्य नान्यथा कुलभूषण! ॥ ४२ ॥

अवश्यमन्नदानेन नियतं तोषयेच्छिवाम् ।
नित्यश्राद्धं तथा संध्यावन्दनं पितृतर्पणम् ॥ ४३ ॥

तथेयं कुलदेवीनां[2] नित्यता कुलपूजने ।
पशुरूपां शिवां देवीं यो नार्चयति निर्जने ॥ ४४ ॥

---

१. चरितमिति तन्त्रसारे २. कुलसेव्यानां

शिवारावेण तस्याशु सर्वं नश्यति निश्चितम् ।
जपपूजाविधानानि यत्किंचित्सुकृतानि च ॥ ४५ ॥

गृहीत्वा शापमापाद्य शिवा रोदिति निर्जने ।
एकया भुज्यते यत्र शिवया देव भैरव ! ॥ ४६ ॥

तत्रैव सर्वशक्तीनां प्रीतिः परमदुर्लभा ।
पशुशक्तिर्नरशक्तिः पक्षिशक्तिस्तथैव च ॥ ४७ ॥

पूजिता विगुणं कर्म सगुणं कारयेत्ततः ।
तेन सर्वप्रयत्नेन कर्तव्यं पूजनं महत् ॥ ४८ ॥

राजादिभयमापन्नो देशान्तरभयादिकम् ।
शभाशुभानि कर्माणि विचिन्त्य बलिमाहरेत् ॥ ४९ ॥

गृह्ण देवि ! महाभागे ! शिवे ! कालाग्निरूपिणि !
शुभाशुभफलं व्यक्तं ब्रूहि गृह्ण बलिं तव ॥ ५० ॥

एवमुच्चार्य दातव्यो बलिः कुलजनप्रियः ।
यदा न गृह्यते वत्स ! तदा नैव शुभं भवेत् ॥ ५१ ॥

शुभं यदि भवेत्तत्र भुज्यते तदशेषतः ।
एवं मत्वा महादेव ! शान्तिस्वस्त्ययनं चरेत् ॥ ५२ ॥

कुलाचारं दक्षिणाख्यं कथितं तव सुव्रत ! ।
न कस्मैचित्प्रवक्तव्यं यदीच्छेच्छाश्वतं सुखम् ॥ ५३ ॥

निर्जने चैव वक्तव्यं न चैव जनसंनिधौ ।
न पितुः संनिधाने वा न मातुः संनिधौ तथा ॥ ५४ ॥

किं वा पक्षिपतङ्गादिदर्शने नैव कारयेत् ।
पातालमण्डपे वापि मण्डपे वा सुयन्त्रिते ॥ ५५ ॥

निश्छिद्रमण्डपे वापि कर्तव्यं न च संनिधौ ।
कुलपुष्पं कुलद्रव्यं कुलपूजां कुले जपम् ॥ ५६ ॥

---

१. °मासाद्य   २. पक्षिशक्तिश्च भैरव   ३. साधयेत्ततः

गुरुं कुलपतिं चापि कुलमालां कुलाकुलम् ।
कुलचक्रं कुलध्यानं सर्वथा न प्रकाशयेत् ॥ ५७ ॥

प्रकाशात् सिद्धिहानिः स्यात्प्रकाशाद्बन्धनादिकम् ।
प्रकाशान्मन्त्रनाशः स्यात्प्रकाशादेव हिंसनम् ॥ ५८ ॥

प्रकाशान्मृत्युलाभः स्यान्न प्रकाश्यं कथंचन ।
पूजाकाले तु देवेश ! यदि कोऽप्यत्र गच्छति ॥ ५९ ॥

दर्शयेद्वैष्णवीं मुद्रां विष्णुन्यासं तथा स्तवम् ।
प्रकाशाद्यदि गुप्तिः स्यात्तत्प्रकाशान्न दूषणम् ॥ ६० ॥

गोपनाद्यदि व्यक्तिः स्यान्न गुप्तिः साभिधीयते ।
कदाचिदङ्गहानिस्तु न च व्यक्तिः कदाचन ॥ ६१ ॥

वरं पूजा न कर्तव्या न च व्यक्तिः कदाचन ।
एतत्तन्त्रं गृहे यस्य कुलाक्षरसमन्वितम् ॥ ६२ ॥

कुलेश्वरलिपिर्वापि तत्रैवाहं सदा स्थिता ।
तेषां गृहेषु पापानि दुष्कृतानि भयादिकम् ॥ ६३ ॥

पुस्तकस्थितिमात्रेण नश्यन्त्यत्र न संशयः ।
लिखित्वा कुलहस्तेन कुलद्रव्येण भैरव ॥ ६४ ॥

कुलवारे पठेद्वापि कुलहस्ते च धारयेत् ।
सर्वथा तस्य [3]गेहं वै न संत्यक्ष्यामि भैरव ! ॥ ६५ ॥

अत्यन्तरोगयुक्तो वा शुभहीनोऽपि वा पुनः ।
एतत्तन्त्रसमायोगात्त्याज्यो न हि कथंचन ॥ ६६ ॥

कुलं कंचित्समालोक्य लभ्यते कुलपूजनम् ।
एतद्ग्रन्थसमायोगात् कपालीकरणं यदि ॥ ६७ ॥

क्रियते साधकेन्द्रेण तदा किं वा न लभ्यते ।
संपूज्य कुलदेवं च गृह्णीयाच्चैव नान्यथा ॥ ६८ ॥

---

१. कुलमानं २. तथा चरेत् ३. देहं

न स्नेहान्न च लोभेन न भीत्या कारणान्न च ।
राज्यहानिर्वरं वापि सुतहानिस्तु वा पुनः ॥ ६९ ॥

वित्तस्य हानिर्वा देव न प्रकाश्यं कदाचन ।
मन्मायामोहितं चापि अन्यदेवरतोऽपि च ॥ ७० ॥

प्रकाशात् क्षोभमाप्नोति सत्यं सत्यं वदाम्यहम् ।
यथा योषिच्छरीरेण विचरामि पुनः पुनः ॥ ७१ ॥

तथेमं ग्रन्थमासाद्य तिष्ठामि परमा कला ।
महाचीनक्रमं वापि महानीलं सदाशिवम् ॥ ७२ ॥

संकेतं वापि योन्मत्तं यत् किंचिद्वीरसाधनम् ।
कुलाचारं विना वत्स नैव सिद्धिप्रवर्तकम् ॥ ७३ ॥

कुलवारे कुलर्क्षे च कुललग्ने कुलक्षणे ।
योगिनीनां सदा पूजा मनसापि न हीयते ॥ ७४ ॥

कुलीनां नावमन्येत नावज्ञां कारयेद्बुधः ।
अभिभूतिसमाकीर्णं व्याधियुक्तं च भैरव ! ॥ ७५ ॥

एतद्ग्रन्थेन [1]निर्मुच्या पिच्छकोपरि धारयेत् ।
सप्ताहं क्रमयोगेन मुक्तो भवति दुर्ग्रहात् ॥ ७६ ॥

एतत्ते कथितं वत्स ! देवीहृदयमुत्तमम् ।
न कस्मैचित्प्रयोक्तव्यं प्रवक्तव्यं कथंचन ॥ ७७ ॥

इदानीं भव सर्वज्ञः सर्वतन्त्रविशारदः ।
त्वमेव वक्ता शास्त्राणां न परोऽपि महेश्वर ! ॥ ७८ ॥

गुरुस्त्वं सर्वतन्त्राणां नाहं नापि हरिः प्रभुः ।
कारणावस्थयापन्ना यद्यहं कुलरूपिणी ॥ ७९ ॥

न कार्यं नापि यत् किंचित् ब्रह्मोऽहं स्फुरितप्रभम् ।
कार्यभावसमापन्ना यदाहं विश्वरूपिणी ॥ ८० ॥

---

१. निर्गच्छेत्पितृकोपं विधारयेत् ।

तदा त्वमेव तन्त्राणां वक्ता नाहं महेश्वर ।
अहं विशामि त्वद्देहे शक्त्या युक्तो भव प्रभुः ॥ ८१ ॥

मां विना जननी कापि नैव कार्यविभाविनी ।
अतः कार्ये समुत्पन्ने पुत्रत्वं त्वयि वर्तते ॥ ८२ ॥

त्वां विना जनकः कोऽपि नैव कार्यविभावकः ।
अतस्त्वमेव जनको नास्त्यन्योऽपि कथंचन ॥ ८३ ॥

कदाचित्पितृरूपोऽसि कदाचिद्गुरुरूपधृत् ।
कदाचित्पुत्रतापन्नः कदाचिच्छिष्य एव हि ॥ ८४ ॥

शिवशक्तिसमायोगाज्जायते सृष्टिकल्पना ।
शिवशक्तिसमायोगात् कुलादेर्मुक्तिकल्पना ॥ ८५ ॥

शिवशक्तिमयं सर्वं यत्किंचिज्जगतीगतम् ।
तस्मात्त्वमेव सर्वत्र सर्वत्राहं महेश्वर! ॥ ८६ ॥

सर्वं त्वमेव देवेश! सर्वं चाहं सनातन! ।
गुरुस्त्वं यदि शिष्योऽहं तदा मास्तु विवेचना ॥ ८७ ॥
तस्माद् भव गुरुर्नाथ शिष्याहं परमेश्वर! ॥ ८८ ॥

॥ इति कुलचूडामणितन्त्रे सप्तमः पटलः ॥

॥ समाप्तश्चायं ग्रन्थः ॥

शोधनम्

Page	Line	
१	१६	योगिनीजालम्
४	६	प्रापयिष्यामि
५	५	ब्रह्मरन्ध्र०
,,	२०	भैरवीभैरवात्मानं
८	२०	आचार्यस्त०
२४	११	ज्ञातव्यः
२५	३	सिद्धिश्चेत्
३०	२१	तत्सहस्रं

श्लोकानुक्रमणिका

भारती विजयम प्रेस, मद्रास-५.